My mate STEVE IRWIN

LIFE BEFORE THE CROCODILE HUNTER

Tony Frisby & Julie Gatehouse

My mate STEVE IRWIN

LIFE BEFORE THE CROCODILE HUNTER

LONGUEVILLE
BOOKS

LONGUEVILLE
BOOKS

First published by
Longueville Books
68 Oxford Street
Woollahra NSW 2025 Australia

www.longmedia.com.au
info@longmedia.com.au
T. + 61 2 9362 8441

First printed October 2009
Second printing November 2009

Cover design: Longueville Media/Nina MB Nielsen

National Library of Australia Cataloguing-in-Publication entry
Author: Gatehouse, Julie.
Title: My mate Steve : life before the crocodile hunter / Julie Gatehouse, Tony Frisby.
Edition: 1st ed.
ISBN: 9781920681487 (pbk.)
Subjects: Irwin, Steve, 1962-2006.
Frisby, Tony.
Friendship.
Herpetologists--Australia--Biography.
Naturalists--Australia--Biography.
Wildlife conservationists--Australia--Biography.
Other Authors/Contributors:
Frisby, Tony.
Dewey Number: 597.9092

The cover shows a croc map drawn by Steve for Tony & Melinda when they went on their honeymoon to Cape York – 'you can't just go on a honeymoon, you've got to look for reptiles!' There is another of Steve's treasure maps on page 178.

Main cover image: taken by the McShanes from the Dalbeg Inn after Steve and Tony caught Bogie the croc at the Burdekin River in North Queensland.

Foreword

Tony, congratulations on your book.

I very much enjoyed reading about those old times. They brought back wonderful memories.

I believe that you have portrayed Steve as a normal, down to earth Aussie bloke, but with a very special talent. As you well know those times swapping stories around the campfire will never be forgotten. If ever I was in trouble out in the scrub, the two mates I would like by my side would be Steve and you.

To have been able to work with you and Melinda in those early years at the zoo and in the field was a great privilege.

Bob Irwin
Wildlife campaigner

About the authors

Tony Frisby is a parks ranger based at Yeppoon in Queensland. His early friendship with Steve Irwin sparked three decades of saving wildlife, from joining Steve and Bob Irwin on reptile-catching trips in remote bush to becoming one of the early curators at the Irwins' reptile and fauna park (now Australia Zoo).

Julie Gatehouse is a Sunshine Coast-based journalist with 19 years' experience in newspapers and magazines. She worked with Tony to write this book.

Contents

Acknowledgements

We would like to thank our families, friends and all others who have contributed to this book either with stories or photographs of their time and memories with Steve.

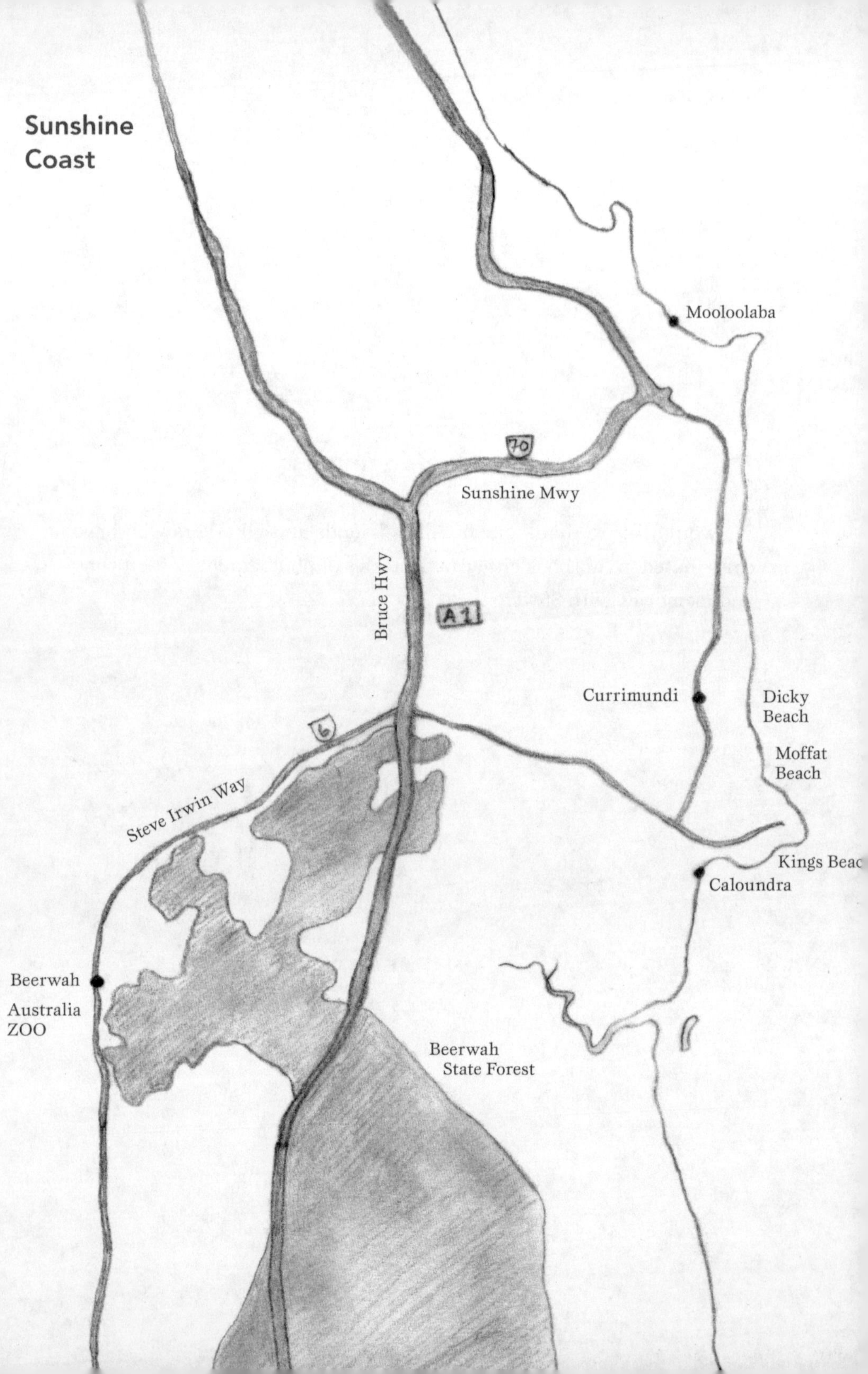
Sunshine
Coast
Mooloolaba
70
Sunshine Mwy
Bruce Hwy
A1
Currimundi
Dicky
Beach
Moffat
Beach
6
Steve Irwin Way
Kings Beac
Caloundra
Beerwah
Australia
ZOO
Beerwah
State Forest

Preface

Best mates to best man

I don't quite know how it all happened. One moment I was laughing with my teenage surfing buddy Stevo as he got hammered by the suckiest waves at Currimundi Beach, the next I was grinning in a best man's suit beside him at his wedding in Oregon.

How did 'having a few beers with my mate' and admiring Stevo's tree-climbing party tricks during a session at Dicky Beach Surf Club become sinking Bundy Rum chasers around a campfire in Cape York after we'd jumped on wild crocodiles?

At what point did our friendship deepen from silly buggers to a trust so deep we regularly risked our lives to ensure the other's safety? And if I'm getting deep, why, oh why, did I once force him to choose between his wife and his best man on a matter of pride?

I watched Steve Irwin morph from my work colleague at Beerwah's struggling little reptile park into the world-famous Crocodile Hunter TV star and face of mega-branded Australia Zoo.

This was a bloke who preferred predators to the public. He gratefully accepted showmanship pointers off me after my stint as curator of a crocodile farm in north Queensland.

We travelled thousands of kilometres to find rare Aussie animals. Steve proudly called us 'the bring 'em back alive team'. I saw him get bitten by a shark while diving and by a croc while feeding it. I kept a wary distance as he played with venomous snakes in the outback and the ocean.

We shared our dreams and our worries. When he cried I tried to be there for him. And when his temper flared I tried not to be!

How lucky was our Sunshine Coast surfie gang to knock around with the real Steve Irwin long before he was playing himself in his own Hollywood movie and hanging around A-listers like Russell Crowe?

I never thought I'd have to ponder these questions in detail. A great mateship is one of those things most Aussie blokes take for granted. (It's like talking about chicks—light on analysis, heavy on action.)

After all, I grew up as a boxer and was more comfortable with fists than words in my thuggish youth. Hypo Stevo could never sit still and had little time for introspection when he was knee-deep in roo poo or chook carcasses for the crocs' dinner.

But that was long before 4 September 2006.

On that day Steve Irwin swam at Batt Reef off the north Queensland coastline while filming a doco for his beloved Bindi. He died doing what he loved, but he left behind all those who loved him.

His family has had to survive their grief in the global spotlight. I can't imagine how impossible that must be for his wife Terri and kids Bindi and Robert.

It breaks my heart to think of the suffering of Steve's father, an awe-inspiring man I called Doctor Bob. Bob showed me on countless occasions why Steve was a chip off the old block.

For myself and my wife Melinda, and other old Sunshine Coast friends who are not connected to the zoo, there has been a surreal quality to our sadness.

When we cry, it's for that funny, frenetic, flesh-and-blood Stevo we grew up with from the 1970s to early 1990s.

It's not for the Steve that has literally become a marble statue (at Mooloolaba), a metal road sign (Steve Irwin Way at Beerwah) and a multi-million dollar public-private partnership (Steve Irwin Wildlife Reserve on Cape York).

There's certainly nothing wrong with tributes and I'm pleased that his celebrity status is working to fulfil his lifelong goal of protecting Aussie wildlife.

But I want the world to meet and appreciate the intriguing bloke known only to our inner circle. Steve Irwin was a boy, a teenager and an adult before he was a husband, a father and an icon. So ordinary, yet so extraordinary. He had flaws like all of us, but his special brilliance attracted us like bloody great moths to a flame.

*

My devastation at Steve's death took me a little by surprise, given that we were living very different lives by 2006. I was a Queensland Parks and Wildlife Service ranger living in Yeppoon, almost 600 kilometres (370 miles) from Beerwah, with Melinda and our two young children Sheyanne and Nathan.

One of the last times I had seen Steve was on a family visit to Australia Zoo on 13 October 2002, when he and Bindi gave three-year-old Nathan and me the rare and dangerous pleasure of joining them in the Komodo dragon enclosure.

I knew the Komodo was one of the world's deadliest animals. Native to Indonesia, this huge monitor lizard harbours poisonous mouth bacteria with no cure. In the wild they eat cattle by biting them on the leg, following them until they drop and then tearing the prey apart. This one was 80 kilograms (175 pounds), easy. If he lunged forward and bit my son or Bindi, they'd be dead. There's no way Steve or I could have restrained him.

Steve was busting to get me near his new Komodo. As I reached out to pat it, my hand shook. I was nervous and I'd had a big night. I'd been to a mate's wedding at Noosa the previous evening and we'd driven directly to the zoo.

Steve said, 'Mate, you don't have to pat it if you don't want to, I can see your hand shaking.'

But that's how much I trusted him: I took my toddler in there with that animal.

Steve calmly talked to Nathan about the endangered creature, proudly pointing out its quiet behaviour. Bindi was only a couple of years older than Natty, but showed incredible maturity and self-confidence. Steve later signed a *Crocodile Hunter: Collision Course* movie poster that still has pride of place in my now nine-year-old son's bedroom.

These visits with Steve could get emotional. When we chatted I'd see tears well up in his eyes and they would in mine, too. It was a spontaneous recognition that we'd enjoyed such a close friendship yet had drawn apart since I left the zoo in 1993, a traumatic period which I'll go into later.

When Steve was killed, I felt shock and black sorrow. Despite more than four decades of pushing the limits, I'd never had anyone close to me die. I grieved not only for a lost mate, but for the potential he could no longer fulfil, the animals' lives he could no longer save. So unfair.

I couldn't bring myself to attend a memorial organised by the old crew on the Sunshine Coast. (We were not invited to the private family funeral.) Instead, Steve's close friend Chris White, now my brother-in-law, sent me the musical DVD tribute he compiled and played at the friends' memorial. It was based on photos taken by another close mate Jeff 'Jibba' Allchin, who was always whipping out the camera as we grew up. You'll share some of the pictures in these pages.

Jibba recalls the spirited afternoon at the Kings Beach Tavern. 'It really showed how many of Steve's old crew remained,' he says. 'We got a couple of hundred people there to show their support. Plenty of funny moments of course, with people wearing creepy crawlies and one guy attaching a blow-up crocodile to his car. We all remembered Steve's humour.'

The DVD's colourful images of our wild and wacky parties and relationships were made poignant by the soundtrack of Steve's favourite songs: Billy Idol's *Rebel Yell*, *I Was Made For Lovin' You* by KISS *and* Iggy Pop's *Real Wild Child*.

The more I poured over my treasured photo albums full of our adventures and chatted to his friends about the good times, the more I wanted to share these memories of Steve.

Initially I didn't know if I had the strength. In fact, the first time I managed to speak about Steve without breaking down was when writer Julie Gatehouse interviewed me for this book at my Yeppoon home. It was a perfect setting for this story. As we sat at my glass dining table with its carved wooden crocodile centrepiece, my son fed his children's python in its nearby aquarium and my Staffie dog Rock begged for food at the door.

The barrage of controversial newspaper, magazine and TV headlines didn't make it any easier: the marketing of Bindi, the way Terri managed the zoo, Bob's departure from the zoo and linked property Ironbark Station, a fight over a mining permit on the Irwin reserve up north. At times I was distracted by fury, particularly when Bob—for whom I have enormous respect—appeared to be in the firing line.

Finally I decided.

A book would help more people understand Steve's motivation, his personality, his genuine spirit. More people could see the fantastic results of his photography obsession, along with my precious photos of our adventures together.

Steve never made it past 44 years old. I've turned 44 and am full of vivid memories.

I could offer fresh insight into the bloke, the surfie, the footy player, the reptile lover, the life of the party, the hard worker, the mate. My mate. A bloke who was into conservation long before the publicity machine dubbed him the Crocodile Hunter. (I've got to say that name never gelled with me. More like Crocodile Whisperer. But what do I know? It made him a fair few bucks!)

So please, just for this book, try to forget the proverbial that hit the fan after that stingray pierced Steve's heart.

Pull up a billy tea and some baked beans and be prepared for a blast from the past as I tell you about my mate, Stevo.

I don't quite know how it all happened, but it was a bloody wild ride.

Chapter 1

Surf 'n' turf with teenage Stevo. Baggie boardies and a bit of biff. 'You know he catches crocs for a living?' You gotta earn and learn respect.

Stevo first hit my radar when I was about 14 or 15 years old. It was the late 1970s and his family had moved up from Melbourne at the start of that decade. He was a couple of years older, but we both hung out with the same group in Caloundra's beachfront suburbs after classes finished for the day at Caloundra State High. Stevo graduated Year 12 in 1979. I left at 15 to start a bricklaying apprenticeship.

Caloundra was a popular weekend holiday spot for tourists from Brisbane. About an hour's drive north of the state capital along Queensland's east coast, it had sunny weather, endless beaches, cheap caravan parks and even cheaper fish 'n' chips and icecream shops. The Caloundra region sprawled from the sandy Pacific Ocean shore to green valleys and craggy mountains in the west. It attracted families who didn't like the glitz, higher prices or highrises on the Gold Coast, an hour's drive south of Brisbane. The 'Brizzoes' called our home the North Coast, now known as the Sunshine Coast.

Of course we locals, better known as townies, generally loathed this weekend menace, and were territorial about our surf breaks.

I stuck with local surfers Stevo and brothers Mick and Chris White. The Whites were family friends of the Irwins and my family, the Frisbys. Stevo and I also played for the same footy club, the Caloundra Sharks, although he was a grade higher than me. We grew to realise we had a lot in common: a love of surfing, diving, rugby league and animals, then later, girls and partying.

Our friendship was cemented when I started spending weekends doing fun stuff with him at his Beerwah home, a reptile park built by his parents Bob and Lyn on 1.6 hectares (4 acres) in 1970. It seemed more like a big, exciting, bush backyard than a commercial tourist enterprise. It had a small enclosure with snakes and lizards, some ponds with a few crocodiles and alligators, plus roaming wallabies. The whole family was passionate about wildlife, particularly reptiles, and it quickly rubbed off on me. I had no idea that nature and conservation would become my life too.

Despite the park facing the old Bruce Highway, the main thoroughfare from Brisbane, it only got a handful of people through the gate each day. Though the Irwins expanded with another 1.6 hectares in 1980, renaming it the Queensland Reptile and Fauna Park, I remember how everyone panicked when the highway bypass was built later that decade. Would people still come?

None of us imagined it expanding into the 28-hectare (70 acre) Australia Zoo gigantor with a million annual visitors by 2008. (And still growing.)

My family lived in suburbia at Diamond Head, Caloundra. We were fairly well-off. My dad John Frisby worked on oil rigs, mainly in Indonesia, and was away a lot. My mum Shirley stayed home to look after me and my younger siblings Mandy, now married to Chris White, and John-Paul, also now married.

My mum was a Thompson, one of the prominent families in Caloundra in the '70s. Midway through the decade about 16,000 residents were spread across the shire's thousand square kilometres and even the commercial centre of town, near our suburbs, had a sleepy reputation. Lots of retirees lived in lowset brick numbers or fibro shacks—with a mango tree out the back, of course. Industries stretched from beachside (retail, construction, tourism) to rural (pineapple, dairy and poultry farms) at the base of the Glass House Mountains.

Mum and my aunties worked at the only shopping centre in town, the BCC in the hilly main street. My primary school mates and I would play the pinnies and have milkshakes at a nearby cafe.

Further up Bulcock Street was a drapery owned by old Mr Comino. Respected and community-spirited, Mannie Comino ran our Caloundra Junior Rugby League Club known as the Gold Tops. He made sure all of our team members had money, shorts and socks. He sewed on all the badges. Established in 1970, the club was honoured by Queensland rugby league king Wally Lewis when he opened its clubhouse on home ground at Plover Parade in 1984.

I walked down Bulcock Street a few years ago and was stunned to hear, 'Tony Frisby! Come here.' It was Mr Comino standing out the front of his shop as he always did, frozen in time. He's still an institution. The changes he must have seen from that footpath in the now-bustling region of 100,000 people.

Local connections not only formed tight bonds in sport and business—they're the reason many of Stevo's friends ended up related!

When Stevo was still at high school and didn't yet have a driver's licence, his mum Lyn regularly drove him the half-hour journey from Beerwah to the Whites' house at Caloundra for the weekend. A bunch of us would get on our pushbikes and ride to different surf locations. If we were lucky, the older and wiser Chris gave us a lift in his Ford Falcon.

If we made it to Currimundi we felt like we were on a surfing safari. Now a mass of housing and shopping precincts, Currimundi in those days was undeveloped oceanfront scrub with a midge-riddled lake and considered remote. To me, it was paradise.

*

I'd had to forge my way into the crew because I was a bit younger and I'd missed some school around Year 8 while my family lived overseas. Little did I know the horrible life lessons that smacked me around in Aberdeen, Scotland would actually help me conquer adolescent testosterone power plays on the Sunshine Coast.

I got beaten up almost every day at school in Aberdeen. They hated Aussies. Accustomed to my comfortable classes and playground at Caloundra State Primary, I was ripe for the picking in rough Scottish schools. There, students spent every day trapped between centrally-heated walls as the weather froze outside. My most vivid memory was of the coat rack hall. That's where all the fights happened. Kids climbed on the racks to cheer and jeer at the fight in the middle of the room. Teachers appeared. Then we'd all split.

I started boxing training. I quickly learnt what to do if someone gave you a hard time. Punch first, ask questions later. Thankfully I got expelled from two schools and Mum and Dad decided it wasn't worth persevering. They stayed. I came back to live with Nan and Granddad in town at Caloundra.

It took me a while to settle down. I remember one guy giving me stick in class. He was one of the hottest surfing juniors out of Caloundra. Still, I hopped up and bopped him. Broke his nose. Nasty. I got sent home.

Next thing I knew, members of the Kings Beach crew were after me. They were a big bunch of surfers, a couple of years older, who ruled this prominent, popular break a couple of suburbs away. 'We're gonna get ya,' I was told.

I remember going home upset and telling Granddad my fears. 'I can't run away from this, I've gotta go down to Kings.' So I did.

No one said boo. I went out for a surf and came back in. Still nothing. I think they expected me to hide. Feud over.

At Currimundi, certain crews sat in certain areas of the surf. I'd paddle out and mind my own business. But if someone dropped in on me I'd give him stick. 'F-off, that was my wave.' I earned my stripes.

My first recollection of Steve Irwin in the crowd was among the Kings Beach crew. He was knocking around with Mick, Chris, Jeff 'Jibba' Allchin and Clive, who I already knew. We'd all lay our surfboards on a particular patch of grass in front of a small stucco building near the sand. We'd buy chocolate milk and bacon and egg sangas for breakfast from the shop under the Rolling Surf Motel.

Stevo was your typical blond-haired surfie with one obvious difference: his boardies. We all wore Quiksilver and Billabong boardshorts, maybe black with coloured diamond patterns, and skin-tight. That was the fashion.

Stevo wore the daggiest, baggiest boardies—massive Hawaiian print ones. Floral. No jocks. He didn't care. Plus he usually sported a messy mullet, regardless of hairstyle trends. We soon learnt that Stevo had nothing to prove and if anyone chipped this solid guy from down south they'd come off second best.

*

Chris White, known as Whitey, has an explanation for Stevo's mop. Chris is now 47, a fire station officer, and married to my sister Mandy. They still live at Caloundra. He met Stevo on his first day of Year 8 in 1975.

'I remember Steve hated his bowl-cut,' says Chris. 'A lot of our mothers cut our hair but, like all of us, he grew the length as he got older. Check out our Caloundra High School photo (page i)—trendy, weren't we? Steve's shirts were always undone, in and out of school. And his boardies were actually unique—his mum Lyn handmade them because she figured buying brand names was a waste of money.

'Steve fitted in okay,' Chris continued, 'though he'd come from Landsborough Primary so he was in the "country kids" group—those who'd come from the more rural schools including Beerwah and Glass

House. Most of us knew each other from Caloundra Primary so the country kids had the fishbowl thing happening. Everyone looked at them. Steve was probably used to it, having moved from Melbourne originally. He was six weeks older than me and our friendship just developed.'

Chris recalls that their focus was sport. 'At first Steve was a handy goalkeeper for Beegee's soccer team—the Beerwah Glasshouse United Club. Even though he was thickset and solid, he was surprisingly agile. Then in Grade 10 he wanted to try rugby league, which Mick and I had been playing since we were seven years old.

'Steve played for the Caloundra Sharks in Grade 11 when I was team captain. He performed very well for a guy who didn't play league and made the Queensland Country Schoolboys trials. He wasn't technically great but he was a powerful tackler and ran all day. I'd play halfback or five-eighth and Steve played second row. He was a very tough bloke to come up against. Unfortunately he did his knee cartilage, which plagued him for years after.

'When Steve was about 14 and hanging around Mick and me, he decided to learn to surf. We'd been in the surf lifesaving nippers and board riding from a young age. That's what you did growing up near such fantastic beaches. My dad was in Dicky Beach Surf Club. Tony's dad was in Metro Caloundra. A lot of our families got to know each other through the surf clubs. Steve's grandparents lived near us at Golden Beach so he had lots of places to stay. His Nanna and Pop were really good fun and Steve's mum, Lyn, looked so much like her mother.

'We grew to realise Steve's obsession with animal welfare and his personal tolerance to pain. Even at 13, he was referring to native fauna by Latin names. It wasn't a frilled-neck lizard, it was a *chlamydosaurus kingii*. I'd say, "Speak English Steve, stop showing off." But I guess to him, it was just like a landscape gardener referring to plant species.

'I think it was Grade 9 when he came to class with his hand wrapped in a white bandage. "What'd you do, Steve?" I asked. "Ah, bloody carpet snake got me in the house." He described how a big scrubby had bit his mum's head when she opened the glass-front cage to feed it mice. It wasn't a major injury but Steve saw red. He raced to help Lyn and the snake latched on to his hand. Pythons are non-venomous but the bacteria in its mouth infected his wound. Steve truly was unafraid of any human or animal. And he didn't mind a scrap with either.'

*

As Chris says, we ended up forming a core group of mates, though I battled the age barrier for a while. I was born on 13 November 1964. Stevo was born 22 February 1962. When I was 15 or 16 and they were 17 or 18 we'd do footy training together. But once footy was finished I couldn't yet hang out at the pub, drinking and smoking. And during the week most of us had to concentrate on jobs. Stevo studied at TAFE in Brisbane to get his diesel mechanic qualifications and worked for Maroochy Shire Council, north of Caloundra.

I was good enough to play two grades above my footy age group because Caloundra didn't have an Under 16 side, only Under 18s. But my mum, still living in Scotland, and my Nan worried that I'd get hurt and wouldn't give permission to my coach.

My solution? I played 'away' games where there were fewer familiar faces watching. My team travelled to grounds at Woodford or Stanley Rivers, south-west of the Sunshine Coast, and turned a blind eye to my age. My performance sealed my status with the older blokes.

We were streetwise, but there were codes of behaviour. Our Kings Beach surfing crew, for example, avoided an older crew from another beach territory. Rumour had it they were into the '70s drugs: acid trips, magic mushrooms, heavy dope. We weren't saints but that wasn't our scene, especially when we heard of guys going crazy or committing suicide.

I became obsessed with boxing and lifting weights. When I was about 17, I won the first Sunshine Coast Junior Bodybuilding title. Stevo was bloody strong, but I never saw him pick up a dumbbell in a gym. He basically developed naturally from work and sport.

One morning a gang of Brizzoes rocked up to the bitumen carpark at Kings Beach. Our turf. They wanted to give us a hard time in the surf. There had been some sort of showdown the night before outside Whiteys' pizza place. Mick and Chris's dad owned the pizza shop in the main street, down the hill from the post office. My cousin Pete Usher was with us.

Pete, who still lives in Caloundra, recalls: 'They were all wearing black T-shirts and jeans. At the beach! We were down in the surf. Stevo's dog Chilli used to sit on the beach and refuse to move if he was surfing. But that morning she was racing back and forwards up to the carpark.'

So we went to see what was going on. Someone was trying to vandalise Stevo's brown Falcon. Stevo walked up, picked up an enormous sandstone rock bordering the carpark and bang! Straight on the bonnet of their car. They all hopped out and bolted. Stevo could be a wild bloke and we made a pretty wild force.

There were lots of biffs over the years but we hated dirty or knife fighters or criminals who robbed people. I don't think we looked for trouble. It was probably a combination of testosterone, youth and alcohol.

A few disputes revolved around a big bloke named Russell who was universally feared. One night he and Stevo had a blue. It was a good one. They went toe-to-toe and Stevo only got a busted eye. The next morning Russell and the lads rocked up at our mate Rod's house, where we often crashed out. They were expecting to see Stevo, but he was the only one not there. Instead, the rest of us outnumbered the visitors. They got a shock and backed down.

Not long after that I was living with a mate also named Russell, but he was a pro-boxer from Brisbane. The two Russells got stuck into it at The Perle Hotel at Kings Beach and for some reason I was involved. Being small, I would never have voluntarily taken on big Russell, but there I was, slugging it out in the drive-through between the bottl'o and the snakepit bottom bar. At least I was left standing.

One memorable night I'd just finished a tough amateur fight in the ring at the Currimundi Pub and sported a massive black eye. In the carpark a guy in a red convertible picked me. So I had to start swinging again. That wasn't much fun.

Looking back, I owe a lot to my future wife Melinda for eventually taming me.

*

Our mate Jibba remembers another colourful moment:

'Tony could fight like a threshing machine,' Jibba says. 'He was a shocker. But he would never pick Steve—though they always played jokes on each other. One night our gang got into an argument with some other blokes at the old Mooloolaba Hotel. It was over a girl. The pub's no longer there but it used to have a drive-through bottleshop and that's where things started. But everyone smiled when Steve stepped up to this guy and goes, "Righteo mate, you and me, out the back."

'Our gang started taunting this guy: "You know the worst thing you could do at this point is hit him? That'll just make him cranky. You know he catches crocs for a living?" The guy's friend went, "Oh shit," and by the time my future wife Sue turned up in a car, the would-be fighter was backing away, real quick. The barney never happened. We jumped in the car and took off before the cops turned up to the ruckus.'

*

As Jibba points out, we always had decent respect for the coppers. It might seem strange but my mates and I were brought up to obey—or was that fear?—our parents and authorities such as police. If we didn't there was hell to pay. When I landed in Caloundra Police Station because someone wanted to put me on an assault charge, the officer declared, 'Righteo. Let's put the gloves on and go for it, Tony. You think you can fight, let's do it.'

'Not a chance,' I said. No way in the world. That officer would have flogged me and I knew that. Lesson learnt. I met him again recently and paid my dues.

When Stevo or Rod visited my house, none of us swore in front of my parents. I'd act the same at their houses. There were untouchable standards for our families and as I started spending so much time with the Irwins, respect was just one of the qualities that sunk in.

Chapter 2

Margarita's, anyone? Tarzan and the towel parties. Don't take yourselves seriously, boys. Bouncing back at cricket. Dares and getting hammered, surf style.

Stevo's weekend antics as a teenager are the stuff of legend among our old gang. A typical weekend would start Friday night at 5 o'clock, happy hour at Margarita's. This small Mexican restaurant at the Golden Beach turnoff could seat 50-odd people and believe me, odd was the right word when we all rocked up at 10 minutes to five for a few beers and something to eat.

Margarita's had a tiny bar area and we would cram in, generally dominating it until 10pm. It was owned by the Hedges and run by the Carneys, two husband-and-wife teams, and it was the best Mexican food on the Coast.

Ninety percent of the crowd was local. Our standard crew would be me, Clive, Stevo, Mick, Rod, Jibba, maybe Chris B, Ross and Gary. Gary was the only one who didn't surf and he had a knee board so we called him The Cripple.

Rugby league was a major talking point because most of us played, or had played, for the Caloundra Sharks. We'd critique and exaggerate our games, which were highly competitive with occasionally vicious results. For some reason Stevo, who was as tall and solid as a tree trunk, always copped the head injuries.

I was only 65 kilograms (143 pounds), but very fit because I boxed on the amateur circuit until my early 20s. My coaches put me in the ring at fights from the Currimundi Hotel to Brisbane's Festival Hall to Mt Isa Civic Centre. I was undefeated in Light Middleweight.

Check out the photo of a memorable footy game (page ii) when some of the Kings Beach guys—me, the White brothers, Jibba, Stevo—took on Moffat Beach. In our favour was the fact that we played in the grades whereas the Moffat boys were surfie bums, really. A few of us, myself included, had also trained and rowed with Metropolitan Caloundra Surf Club so when we played Moffat we caned them. That's the way it was.

Jibba remembers playing with Stevo in reserve grade: 'He was so gungho, he just ran straight into people.'

After Margarita's our group would head off to either the Currimundi Pub or The Perle, a pretty rough joint that's since become the fancy Kings Beach Tavern—nice to see the owners have kept a slice of history by naming a room The Perle Bar.

Or we'd hold crazy costume parties at our houses. Stevo would always put a lot of thought into his fancy dress. As a clown he wore a green floral shirt, red braces, a black bowtie and half a pineapple on his head and painted his face white with red diamonds around his eyes and a massive red smile. As a rubbish bin he wore, well, garbage. He played a wicked devil too.

Most of us guys were footloose and fancy free—or desperate, depending on circumstances—and we usually managed to attract a bevy of lovely ladies. The few serious girlfriends in those days displayed great tolerance.

Our twenty-firsts were all wild nights. Stevo's was a dual birthday party for him and Gary. We had a mega fancy-dress do at our gang's party house just off the main street of Caloundra. Jibba, who got great snaps, recalls:

'There was this old fibro Queenslander on a corner block of Bombala Terrace that several of the guys rented over the years. Sad that it's gone now but probably no surprise. Our rule was that all parties were held there. I went to lots of birthdays, New Year's celebrations. If you were lucky—or unlucky—enough to be living there or a regular visitor, typical preparations involved locking the bedroom doors, dragging the lounges to the backyard, setting up the clawfoot bathtub with ice for the beers, and watching dozens of people roll in.

'For Steve and Gazza's twenty-first there was this slab of cake that the girls were very proud of. When the birthday boys bent down to blow out the candles, Steve declared there wasn't enough cake for everyone and Gazza pushed Steve's head in the icing. Well, it was on. This hell food fight just got worse, chunks of watermelon, chips, everything went flying. It was only when rain started pouring that everyone scattered. The girls were ticked off. It had been quite a flash cake.'

Jibba remembers when towel parties were the rage. 'Guests had to come only wearing towels. If you were smart and didn't want your towel yanked off, you put buttons on it. Same deal with shirt parties. The girls bought these long shirts and wore them with belts.

'Steve became infamous for his crocodile undies. His mother had bought him these undies with some sort of Tarzan, croc-wrestling pictures on them. It was the sort of thing I didn't need to know but these undies often made an appearance at parties. Steve wasn't shy when surrounded by friends to impress.

'Drunks from the pub would try to crash our parties so we always needed a couple of blokes out the front as security. Although, at the shirt party, security told three birds and a bloke they could come in if they obeyed the dress code. We were stunned when these three drop-dead-gorgeous girls removed their skintight jeans and walked into the party with their jeans folded neatly over their arms.'

Chris White remembers organising everyone to put a couple of bucks each in a kitty every week to stock up for fun at the old house. 'We threw a couple of legendary New Year's parties,' he says. 'Pigs on the spit, grog supplied. We charged entry and fined people if they weren't in fancy dress. It was well-catered, for a bunch of surfie idiots. Then Jeff and I started the Christmas Eve party tradition at The Perle. It snowballed. Now my daughter enjoys the tradition at what's become the Kings Beach Tavern.'

*

A typical night at Margarita's (Stevo, second on left at front).

The couple in the hot seat at Margarita's during those steamy couple of years were the cooks, Di and Rob Schwenke. Working under chef Paul Ryan, they all fed us spicy Mexican food while forging close friendships and partying just as hard when finished in the kitchen.

'It was 1981 and Rob and I were in our mid to late 20s,' Di recalls. 'We'd been travelling and lobbed on the Sunshine Coast, intending to meet our friends and then head north. But we didn't leave. There was nothing much in Caloundra for young people at that time so Margarita's became the spot. It was more like a watering hole than a restaurant and full of great times.'

Rob remembers 'a tight unit' of 30 or more guys and girls arriving 'ready to rock 'n' roll at 5pm' on weekends. The place would get so packed that it was standing room only. Guys would be leaning on diners' tables, talking and drinking. People eating would ask the kitchen, 'Can you get these people off our tables? What sort of place is this?'

Well, it was a loud place. There was no single ringleader but people tried to outdo each other. And the music speakers were above the servery window, so the kitchen staff would torment the waitresses because they couldn't hear instructions about orders or tables.

'Fris, Irwin, the Whiteys, Ryany, Jib, Johno, Rod, Clivey, Brucey, they were larrikins and you couldn't help but like them,' remembers Rob. 'They were a great bunch of characters and you'd laugh all night with them. Their tomfoolery was the classic Aussie sarcastic humour. It meant don't take yourself seriously.'

*

Margarita's sponsored an indoor cricket team, which became another social event.

'Irwin was a good indoor cricketer,' says Rob Schwenke. 'He was keen, bowled fast and had strength. One night a big bloke put a couple of bouncers into him. Steve goes, "Do that again and you're in trouble." Next thing, the bowler was running for his life, straight out of the cricket centre, with Steve chasing him.

'Another night Steve arrived at cricket with his arm blown up twice its size. This was just after Tony Frisby's twenty-first at the junior leagues club. The boys had stayed up all night but Steve had to leave at 8am to go and feed all the park's snakes. He told us the huge Reticulated python threw itself at the chook he was carrying and wrapped around his arms. He was so tired he couldn't get it off and had to yell for help. His mum and dad unwound it from his neck.

'Yet another night, when we were on the jungle juice at our place after indoor cricket, Steve went riding on his pushbike. You could hear his bell ringing all around Currimundi. Then he borrowed Di's pushbike.'

Di remembers the bike coming back—'with two flat tyres. Steve reckoned he was doing some all-terrain thing. Everyone else would be content having a few drinks and laughs but Steve always had to do something acrobatic.'

But Steve's tree-climbing made the Schwenkes nervous. 'When Di and I started our own restaurant Aztec Gardens at Mooloolaba, he would get merry and climb these tall coconut trees near the surf club, pulling down coconuts to the amazement of our al fresco diners,' says Rob. 'We'd say, "Okay Steve, you can come down now." They were innocent times. Everyone just cruised along, happy go lucky. A fantastic era.'

*

The local surf lifesaving clubs were regular hangouts. They weren't much to look at—not like the swank pokie-funded establishments these days—but they were right on the beach and usually packed.

I would train at a gym downstairs at the Dicky Beach club during the day then tie one on upstairs, where they had a bar and a dancefloor, at night. We guys didn't like dancing but we loved the '80s music. The Angels. INXS. Midnight Oil.

One night a couple of us bored blokes standing at the urinal issued a dare to Stevo. 'Bet you can't jump out the window and grab that tree.'

It was a ridiculous dare. The urinal was on the second storey of the Dicky Beach clubhouse. The toilet window was tiny, long and narrow. This big tree grew up from beside the front door.

Without further ado Stevo clawed his way through the frame, his fingers clutching the inside of the sill, and pushed off from the wall with his feet. He leapt and latched on to the tree. If a branch had snapped...

'You're a lunatic,' we decided. I think he got a beer for it.

The dumb stuff we did in cars doesn't bear thinking about in hindsight. No one cared about seatbelts or roadworthiness. Random breath testing for drink-drivers didn't start in Queensland until 1988. A lot of us are lucky to be alive today.

However one of my enduring images of Stevo is him doing a 'Fonzie' behind the wheel of his dented white Honda Accord. You'd never miss him driving past. He always had one hand on the wheel and the other waving crazily as he half-hung out the window shouting 'Heyyyy'. Sometimes guide posts got in the way.

Jibba, as the elder of our group, was the first one to get a car. Another student of Caloundra State High, he also lived at Golden Beach, which became very convenient for getting all of us from home to beach.

Jibba recalls, 'My older sister was friends with Steve's older sister, Joy. I started hanging around with Steve and the group about 1978 when I got my white 1974 Mazda Capella. I named it after the Cherry Venture because it had more rust than the shipwreck up near Double Island Point. The cargo ship had become a tourist attraction after running aground in bad weather in 1973 on its way to Brisbane. (The wreck was removed in 2007.) I suspect the rust had something to do with Steve and me draping our saltwater-soaked boardies over the rearvision and side mirrors, trying to get them dry after a surf.

'The Whites lived in the same street as me, Coronation Avenue, and Steve's grandparents lived nearby at Onslow Street. If Steve stayed at his grandparents' place on Friday night, at 6am on Saturday I'd hear 'knock knock' on my bedroom window. 'Currimundi looks good Jibba, let's go eh?'

'"Okay Steve." I'd grab my board and car keys. We first knew Tony as a kid riding around on a pushbike. He and Clive rode their bikes to the beach to surf. We all formed a solid group when Tony was old enough to get his licence and a little blue Laser from his parents. That's when he and Steve started hanging out more and getting close.'

*

On Saturdays we generally had three options:

1. helping out at the Beerwah park;
2. some form of sport—surfing, footy, diving—and recovery; or
3. going away camping.

Often when we'd get on it the previous night Stevo would hit us up. 'Oh guess what we're doing at the park tomorrow, boys?' It might be chopping down a towering tree out the front or it might be 'we need to move one of the snakes'.

We always said, 'Yeah, all right.'

In fact, one of the first big crocodiles into the park was a result of these 'mates' rates' (six-packs of cold bevvies were acceptable currency). It was even filmed for the Channel 7 news, that's how curious crocs were in south-east Queensland at that time.

I remember helping Bob, Stevo and a few of our mates lift it out of a Pantec truck one sunny day about 1983. The saltie had been caught by local police at Bamaga, right on the northern tip of Cape York, and kept in the prison grounds there for a week before transportation.

The only calm one was Bob. The rest of us put on a brave front, standing beside this monster. Some of us weren't even wearing shirts, let alone protective gear. We were packing death. It was the first time I'd been so hands-on with a wild predator that size. It was amazing to watch those jaws open wide as it stalked out of the wooden crate on to the grass beside its new waterhole. I had no idea that I'd soon be wrapping myself around living, breathing crocodiles while trying to save them from dangers in their own environment.

*

Stevo became renowned for his hyperactivity, even when we were just chilling out. When he came over to our regular sessions at Rod's place at Currimundi, he couldn't just sit around, have a beer or a cup of coffee and do nothing.

He'd say, 'C'mon guys, let's go! I'm going down to surf. Are you just going to sit here? What's going on?'

On and on he chattered. I never saw him sit and watch a video. He'd be walking around, out the back, playing with the dog. You'd be trying to watch the footy on a Friday night or Sunday afternoon but he'd have the dog jumping on the lounge or catching a ball.

So many times we'd all wake up with hangovers and Stevo would be gone. For all we knew, he'd left for north or west Queensland on a bizarre animal-catching errand for his dad. Or we'd struggle down the beach and there he'd be, out on his board.

He'd paddle out there alone, take off on the biggest wave ever and just get smashed. Other guys refused to go out in such rough surf, especially at low tide near what we called the Dicky Beach reef. Stevo would be out there happily, missing takeoffs, getting hammered. Currimundi was his favourite surf spot and he loved Wurtulla Beach too.

Most surfers had a healthy respect for the sharks in our waters. There were plenty of bull whalers in the rivers and tigers in the ocean and each year a great white or two would get caught in the nets or drumlines (baited hooks) which protected our flagged swimming zones. Each spring you knew to watch out for the big sharks chasing the humpback whale calves travelling south with their mums after the breeding season.

I knew one bloke who wasn't so cautious.

Chapter 3

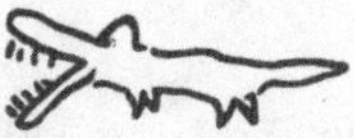

Shark bites man—but man starts it. He Who Must Be Obeyed. Animal house. Love and quirks in the Irwin family.

Scuba diving off Caloundra's sandy beaches was a favourite pastime, and not without its share of dangers. One Saturday the ever-instructional Stevo was explaining to Jibba and me how wobbegong sharks could bite their own tails. We had spotted one, about 1.5-metres (5-feet) long, at Wurtulla rocks. Mate, they are one ugly shark. Flat-headed with brown patterns on top and whiskers sticking out from their mouths, wobbies are bottom-dwellers with fantastic camouflage.

Jibba had seen crayfish behind an underwater ledge. Only problem was, this shark was in front of the crays. Stevo offered to remove it. He dived down, grabbed it by the tail and tried to pull it out. It whipped around and had a chop at him.

When he released its tail the shark must have been pissed off because it came back and bit him twice on the flipper. When a wobby chomps, its mouth locks on. It has heaps of teeth. You need pliers, bloody screwdrivers, to get it off.

Stevo tried to kick it off but this thing gave his flipper a mighty hard chew before it swam away. Despite bleeding toes, he laughed at the lesson learnt as we told him, ‘You’re crazy, you stirred it up!’

*

When I was about 20, Stevo and I camped on Fraser Island to go surfing, snorkelling and diving. A couple of hours’ drive north of the Sunshine Coast and a barge ride across from Rainbow Beach, Fraser is the biggest sand island in the world. It’s more than 120 kilometres (75 miles) of white sand cliffs, pure freshwater lakes and plenty of dingoes.

After an outcry in the 1970s they stopped sandmining there and now it’s tourism gold with World Heritage listing and multi-star resorts. Back then there were far fewer visitors and most of us arrived in old four-wheel-drives with tents and Eskies.

Stevo had a special spot at Ngkala Rocks on the remote north-eastern stretch of the island, facing the open ocean. Freezing westerlies were blowing us inside out—they must have been 15 to 20 knots—but winter was the best time for clear water. Stevo wore a steamer wetsuit and I had my longjohns on.

We jumped in and it was as beautiful as it was cold. Sunlit water peeled off the top of the waves and blew into my face. Below the choppy surface was a set of coffee rocks and soft corals. It may not have had the colourful, hard corals of the Great Barrier Reef up north, but I had never seen so many crayfish and bream swimming around me. How Stevo kept it a secret for that long, I don’t know.

We started spear fishing for dinner. Let me interrupt at this point to say yes, we knew the ocean side of Fraser Island, like Moreton and Stradbroke islands just to the south, was notorious for big sharks. Just about everyone who lives in south-east Queensland does. And yes, dragging bleeding fish about when you look like a seal could be perceived as risky. Especially when it’s the season for mullet and tailor, which travel close to shore to feed on bait fish and in turn attract more sizeable predators. But I took my lead from fearless Stevo and our surfing culture, which relied on gut instinct and statistics showing very few attacks on humans over the years.

We were busy collecting crayfish when I realised Stevo was standing, balanced, on a half-submerged rock.

I didn't take much notice and kept swimming around.

I didn't realise he was yelling, and had been for a while. I'm deaf in one ear. Finally he got my attention and I understood what he was shouting.

'Hey Fris! Hey! Hey! Big shark out here.'

My stomach dropped. Damn it Steve, you coulda told me earlier!

'Okay so we're going in then?' I said.

'Nah,' he said. 'It's a big fella, but it'll be right. It'll stay out the back there.'

Um, I didn't think so. I took off, straight back to the beach.

Stevo pottered around a while longer. He just didn't care. I think it was only the cold that forced him back to shore.

As we walked up to the headland I finally saw the size of the shark, which was still cruising back and forth.

About a dozen feet long (3.5 metres). Bloody hell.

That night Stevo cooked a great smorgasbord of pippis, crays and fish on our campfire. I remember it distinctly because it tasted horrible when it came back up. I wish we'd gone easier on the pre-dinner beverages. As my wife Melinda says, it took us far too long to learn not to waste good meals like that.

Double Island Point, south of Rainbow Beach, was another of our preferred places to surf and camp. Stevo would chat about his father-son fishing trips to reefs off the Sunshine Coast. He and Bob often spent days on their 17-footer (5-metre boat) fishing places like Barwon Banks, about 40 kilometres (25 miles) offshore and known for snapper, pearl perch and sweetlip. I admired their special relationship.

*

I watched Stevo grow to emulate his dad: Bob's thirst for knowledge, his commanding demeanour. Although the junior Irwin was louder and more reckless.

Bob Irwin was slight and short compared to his son, but he was a very fit middle-aged man and never carried any weight. Bob slogged away from daybreak to dusk. He wore a pair of Stubbies shorts and old boots with a button-up shirt undone almost to the waist. A rollie was fixed to the corner of his mouth.

One arm was a bit bung where he'd been grabbed by a croc; he'd been bitten by venomous snakes too. We suspected he'd cop some sort of organ failure as he aged due to all the toxins. But he's now pushing 70, healthy and still working his guts out for wildlife.

From Stevo's teen years on, he referred to his dad as He Who Must Be Obeyed. I knew him as Doctor Bob. Bob's physical presence may have been unimposing but his wisdom was infinite and you would never, ever doubt him. He had an aura.

Every time we spoke to Bob, he'd be sitting calmly, rolling a cigarette and listening intently. Then he'd start explaining. He rarely raised his voice, though you knew if he wasn't happy. Not that he wasn't happy with me often—I don't think. Bob's instructions were crystal clear and you followed them to the letter. You knew he would be right.

Doctor Bob's world revolved around caring for wildlife and nature. He was self-taught in animal welfare and husbandry and we all gained hands-on experience out of necessity; the park simply couldn't afford to hire vets or scientists or researchers at the drop of a hat.

I'm glad Bob's herpetology expertise is now widely recognised. (Herpetology is the study of reptiles and amphibians.) Leaving his beloved zoo in early 2008 in difficult circumstances is now a new beginning. He's created a 260-hectare (640 acre) wildlife reserve and release site near Kingaroy, north-west of the Sunshine Coast, to provide a refuge for orphaned and rehabilitated fauna. He's joined forces with the Royal Society for the Prevention of Cruelty to Animals (RSPCA) in Queensland to educate children. In February 2009 he turned the sod on a new joint project to transform a disused jail at Wacol in Brisbane into a huge new RSPCA wildlife hospital and animal shelter. Not to mention his ongoing work with scientific studies across Australia, namely turtles and wombats. My admiration runs deep.

But if Bob was the king, his wife Lyn shared the crown. Stevo's mum was a tough but brilliant lady, who ruled with an iron fist. She had been a maternity nurse and she knew her stuff like you wouldn't believe.

She specialised in rehabilitating sick or injured birds and macropods—kangaroos, wallabies—and park staff constantly sought her advice. If Lyn suggested a different treatment, environment or diet, she would be proven correct as the animal recovered. Even Bob would say, 'Go see Lyn' if someone turned up carrying an injured possum.

Stevo resembled Lyn, but she was shorter and had a softer build than husband and son. She wore baggy shorts and Jesus-creeper sandals. She usually had a ponytail and the only times I remember her wearing makeup were at my wedding and at Stevo's wedding.

Lyn was a homely, family-oriented lady who loved her two daughters and her Steven, as she called him. She cooked all the cakes for sale at the kiosk but still found time to make us sandwiches or hot dogs every day. None of us paid for lunch at the park.

*

Our mate, Chris White recalls Lyn's delicious baking and generosity, even when surrounded by the chaos of the Irwin household on the park grounds.

'In the early days the Irwins kept all their valuable animals in and around their home,' Chris says. 'It was low-set, dark brick and open-plan. When Steve's mates stayed the night, we'd have to negotiate cages of snakes along the hallway near the bedrooms. I remember the deadly Fierce snake. Sugar gliders flew near the ceiling and Tawny frogmouths kept watch from the rehab cage just outside.

'At that time the three kids were still living at home and you can imagine the arguments—one boy in between two independent girls. It was a typical family, like mine, and no one ever just sat around. Lyn was always baking biscuits and cakes and the smell was unbelievable. Steve brought the best food to high school and breakfast was awesome at his place.

'When Steve and I were about 16 we earned money picking tobacco on a farm near the park so I basically lived with the Irwins when the season was on. Of course Lyn stocked us up with great lunches. Steve was KISS-crazy and had the posters on his bedroom wall. First KISS, then the Steve Miller Band and Billy Idol were his favourites. I'll never forget the crazy rides to and from this tobacco farm on Steve's Honda CB100 motorbike. It had a white petrol tank with blue and red pinstripes. As soon as you left the Irwin garage you had to duck or the house emu would peck you on the back of the head!

'I wasn't as obsessed with animals as the Irwins or Tony or my brother. Maybe it was because I'd seen the legacy of injuries. Did I mention the scar on Steve's wrist from the time he was up a tree with a lace monitor's jaws locked down like a pig dog? Or the blood pouring from welts on Bob's back after a roo went ballistic at the park and kicked him? That one shocked me because I didn't think hand-reared wallabies or kangaroos could be aggressive. Steve raced to the rescue again, punching the roo to stop it attacking his dad. They refused to put it down, of course, but it never played up again.'

*

Chris is right—I became as fascinated by animal welfare as Lyn, Bob and Steve. Lyn could be abrupt if she felt an animal was at risk, such as when a member of the public brought her a sick joey in a plastic bag which could have suffocated it. Friends and strangers were always dropping off wildlife, such as kookaburras and koalas hit by cars.

At first I assumed that human intervention was always needed: see what's wrong with the patient, encourage it to eat, give it medication. I quickly learnt from Bob and Lyn that, 'No, Tony, don't touch it,' was the first step. Then maybe offer water and warmth. Next judge its condition. As my education expanded, I realised that fussing with a hurt animal can make things much worse—even kill it—because of the extra stress on its immune system.

The park had a special enclosure for injured wildlife to the left of the front gate. I liked Curley the one-legged curlew. This bird didn't care that he had to hop around on one long spindly leg. Curley still liked his meat treats and made those ungodly curlew cries at night.

Stevo didn't have a lot of time for birds, but he loved the park's rehabilitated wedge-tailed eagle, Australia's largest bird of prey with a wingspan of more than 2 metres (6.5 feet). This wedgie had an individual cage and a personality to match.

We were forever cleaning this cage. It had deco (decomposed granite) on the floor and we'd have to rake up leaves and the pellets that raptors regurgitate. The wedgie would watch us, fly down, hop over to the pile, grab some of it in his talons, fly to the top perch, and fling them down one at a time. 'Hah, clean my cage will ya?' he taunted.

I think Stevo spoilt him when we were out of sight because this wedgie was obsessed. When Stevo walked into the cage the bird would flirt, making this 'whishoo whishoo' noise.

But my favourite part was when the wedgie got all touchy-feely with the object of his desire. First he would land on Stevo, clinging to his brown Akubra. Then the heavy, razor-taloned bird would try to mate with Stevo's head. Hilarious. Stevo didn't love him that much.

Lyn worked the front counter so she always had baby animals hanging around for feeding. And I do mean hanging around. She made pouches by folding towels and pinning them so they could be slung over the backs of the seats.

She plucked kangaroos from the pouches at toilet time and let them scratch around on the grass. They would jump back to her and claw at her legs, seeking comfort. It was beautiful. I think most of the female roos in the park were handraised.

The enclosure later had to be removed due to government rules designed to protect people from the distress of seeing imperfect animals. But the care continued. That was the precursor to the $5 million wildlife hospital—reportedly the world's biggest facility—now operating at the zoo. It all started with Lyn's magic.

Both husband and son idolised her, which was why her death in a single vehicle accident west of the Coast in 2000 at age 58 almost broke them. Bob told the ABC TV show *Australian Story* in April 2008 that he had been close to suicide when Lyn died. He said a phone call from Steve stopped him.

Steve had previously spoken of his own devastation at his mum's passing (in the same month as their mutual birthday—February). When the Lyn Irwin Memorial Fund was set up, Steve wrote (on www.australiazoo.com.au): 'I've been busted up, smashed up, hospitalised…but the pain of losing my Mum is unbearable and relentless…She was the Mother Teresa of wildlife, a saint, and she will be remembered forever…Every single day she worked and toiled to save injured and orphaned joeys while maintaining a happy, healthy, Irwin clan…I've adopted your strength, your passion and enthusiasm…I love you, I miss you, I long to be reunited with you.'

I struggle with the fact that Steve and I never sat down for a quiet chat about it all. At the time there had been so much water under the bridge and we were living separate lives. I wanted to be supportive, but had no idea what to say. None of us had much practice discussing emotions like that. To this day, Bob and I only talk about the good times with Steve and Lyn.

*

The Irwins were a devoted family. How many families of five can live, work and play together for any length of time?

Stevo's kid sister, Mandy, worked at the kiosk, but I rarely saw her. She preferred horses to reptiles and was often away at equestrian events.

Stevo had no time for Mandy's horses. He cursed them for digging up the turf and nibbling on his palm trees. When he mowed, the horses would canter all over the place and spook the kangaroos.

Before Main Roads bypassed the highway from the park's front door, cars that drove past with loose tarps flapping on their trailers would send both horses and roos into a frenzy. Roos would bounce off fences and we worried they'd hurt themselves. Then the peacocks would go off. Mate, it was a zoo.

Sometimes Stevo and Mandy's exchanges became heated. He Who Must Be Obeyed would settle down the siblings, acknowledging that Mandy was allowed to have what she wanted too—fair's fair. As Mandy grew up and formed her own opinions and friends, Lyn would have to inform protective Big Brother that his sister's love life was none of his business.

Stevo's older sister Joy dated and married a man named Frank, who is now general manager of Australia Zoo. I didn't have a lot of dealings with Joy at the park, but her two children Rebecca and James were obviously the apples of their grandparents' eyes. Little Bec later took the role of flower girl and walked down a church aisle towards Stevo, me and Mick at Stevo's wedding in Oregon (USA) in 1992.

Of all the wild times I shared with Stevo the best were our trips away, either with his dad or just the two of us. And when I say away, I mean thousands of kilometres, from the desert heat of Queensland's far south-western corner to the lush rivers far west of Maryborough in central Queensland to the rainforests and beaches on the north-eastern tip of Australia. These brutal, beautiful environments set us on a path for life.

Cape York Region

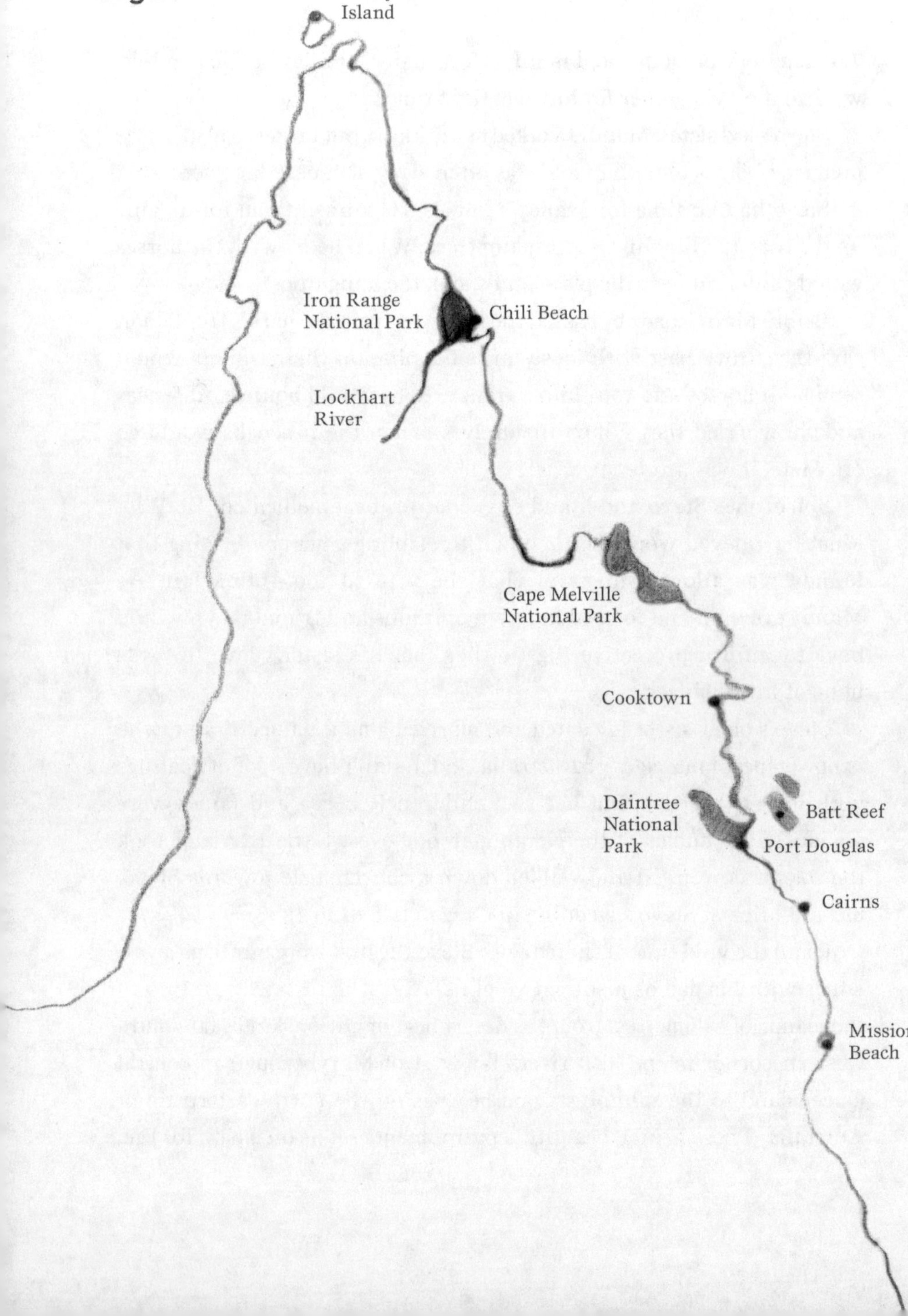

Chapter 4

Now that's fishing. Silent Bob. On the skids. Stevo, help! Sweating in a goanna graveyard. Bodgy budgie photo opp. Don't get snaky, Stevo.

When Stevo and I 'went bush', it meant we were in search of animals: rare and common; flying, slithering and swimming; vicious and harmless. (Not many of the latter.) And we had damn fine times pursuing them. Scary. Hilarious. That's where I saw the Irwin intuition work wonders and I learnt the absolute power of our native animals and environment. Not to mention the hangover power of beer o'clock by the campfire.

In the early '80s Bob, Stevo and I travelled several times to Dawson River, west of Maryborough and near Taroom in central Queensland, to go fishing.

That didn't mean throwing a line off a jetty and sitting idle. No outing was normal or lazy with the Irwins.

Bob had his eye on a pile of saratoga. Also known as the Spotted barramundi, it's an aggressive, freshwater fish native to that area and weighing up to 4 kilograms (8.8 pounds). Dark on top with a white belly, it's covered in little reddish dots. Bob wanted the saratoga to breed in the ponds at the park as cheap, available crocodile food and natural cleaners. He figured he could also target the Asian market for aquarium fish.

We camped right on the edge of Nathan Gorge. It has a steep 150-metre (490-foot) descent best described as a goat track. First we went to the bottom to set the fish traps. At the top we prepared 44-gallon drums full of dam water in the back of the truck, to store the saratoga for the six-hour return drive.

The process was: catch the fish, get them out before they drowned or got damaged, wrap them in cloth in our arms and literally run them up to the truck. It was very, very hard. Sure we lost a couple of fish, but as soon as the drums were full we drove back to Beerwah as quickly as we could.

We never did things the easy way because we didn't have enough money for fancy equipment. We had a cheap blow-up boat from a department store and a panel full of putty on Stevo's battered truck.

In those days cluey Bob—the plumber who became the herpetology guru—was always finding ways to keep the park in the black. His son was his willing protégé. I was addicted to the excitement and experiences. I loved learning about wild animals and the bush. It certainly beat slogging away at my trade of bricklaying, although I didn't get the rainy days off!

Every time we got a chance to sit with Bob and drain his wisdom, we grabbed it. He had a profound respect for and knowledge of native flora and fauna but he wasn't the sort of fella who would volunteer yarns around the campfire. You'd have to milk him for information. So I worked on quiet Bob.

If Bob was sitting there staring, it wasn't a dreamy or glazed look. He'd be analysing something, wondering why a tree grew a particular way, for example. Or he'd be watching the fish traps to make sure no turtles got caught.

Stevo's old man taught us how to think like an animal in order to understand it. The animal's welfare always came first, even at our expense. He would drum into us: when you're working with animals, do it hard and fast to minimise their stress. Bugger your stress levels, you'll live! Enclosures had to suit the animals, not the handlers.

Half the time we ended up like wild animals ourselves—and probably resembled them. Stevo was like a great orang-utan, with his massive meaty hands, solid chest and incredible strength, shinnying up trees. There wasn't a rock he couldn't push, a tree he couldn't climb—and he wouldn't stop at the first branch, he'd reach the top.

Human Orang-utan: there wasn't a tree Stevo couldn't climb—even when setting up a heavy bag trap, Cattle Creek, mid '80s.

However, very quickly we learnt the prophecy of another common Bob refrain—'With animals if it can go wrong, it will go wrong.'

Our fishy gifts from those Nathan Gorge trips were received with pleasure by the park's residents: saltwater crocs Anvil and Monty, two American alligators we called the Fang sisters and three freshwater crocs including one large male named Mr Freshy. We started building special digs for the crocodiles as the Irwins prepared for an ambitious breeding program that would be the clincher to the park's success and Stevo's unbelievable career.

*

At that stage lizards were still the main game for the Queensland Reptile and Fauna Park and I had my first—and hopefully last—confrontation with a perentie, Australia's equivalent of the Komodo dragon.

Stevo had told me we needed to fetch some monitor lizards (goannas) and snakes native to the arid south-western corner of Queensland. He neglected to mention until the last minute that we would be operating in perentie country.

You get an idea of a perentie's size from its scientific name: *varanus giganteus*. Australia's biggest lizard at over 2 metres (6.5 feet), it has a forked tongue, clawed feet on powerful legs and is very territorial. But when I found myself terrified and trapped in a lair, Stevo was there to save my bacon.

We were aiming for Bedourie, a remote border town surrounded by sparsely-vegetated blacksoil plains, between the Simpson Desert and a cattle property that became Diamantina National Park in 1992.

It was stinking hot and the flies were thick. Plagues of them buzzed in the corners of my eyes, ears and mouth when I tried to speak or eat. Sheep wandered the wide, open escarpment searching in vain for grass, instead chewing on rocks like all-day suckers. Then they'd drop dead. I had flashbacks to my early childhood stints in the Simpson Desert and Surat Basin where Dad drilled for oil. Drought in the Aussie outback is a horrific killer.

First on Stevo's list were Spencer's monitors; quiet, beige-coloured, cat-sized lizards. Coming close second on his to-do list and number one on my danger list were Fierce snakes.

These inland taipans are a couple of metres long, thin, bronzey-brown and, you guessed it, the most toxic snakes in the world. The fact that no adult human fatality has been recorded from a Fierce snake is due to its timidity rather than lack of venom. Yet there we were, seeking out its hideyholes. Apparently it could kill an adult human within 45 minutes. We were hours from an emergency department. Mobile phones didn't exist and CB radio didn't always transmit.

Nearing Bedourie from the east, we stopped to check out small monitor lizards and catch snakes off the side of the road. We resumed driving. 'There's one!' I yelled.

Stevo hit the skids, nodding. 'That'll be a Spencer.' Even doing 100 kilometres an hour he would stamp on the brake. We'd both brace as the truck slid—often turning 90 degrees—then in a cloud of dust we'd throw open both doors and bolt out.

He ignored the handbrake and the truck rolled an extra 30 metres or so down the road. We were too late. The goanna escaped into a culvert.

Despite our best attempts to bash our way in, using crowbars and sledgehammers, we gave up after half an hour and moved on. Chancing upon a narrow, muddy tributary of the Georgina River, we figured on fish for dinner. We swam a net across the river, sat under a eucalypt and had a beer.

Out of nowhere, a car pulled up. It was a copper. Out here!

'How are ya, boys?'

'Hey mate. Just getting a feed for tea, you know,' we said.

'Boys, you can't net these rivers without a permit.'

'Oh all right, we'll get it out.'

Hell, we'd thought we were in the uninhabited wild west. Another lesson learnt, and beans for tea before rolling out our swags for the night.

The next morning we drove into Bedourie. It had a school, a council yard and an all-in-one, pub-servo-post office. I asked a Murri lad whipper-snipping some grass what time the fuel pumps opened. He said the lady who owned the servo wouldn't open for hours. 'So how far to the next fuel stop?' I asked.

'Not far, just up the road,' he confirmed.

We risked it, on half a tank with 20 litres in a jerry can in the back. We drove for a long, long time. Things were getting strained but Stevo was determined to keep going until we got to 'the rocks on the side of the road' that Bob had marked on our map.

'What sort of rocks?' I asked.

'Dad said you can't miss 'em,' he replied matter-of-factly.

We finished the jerry can and were just about out of fuel when a homestead appeared like a mirage. After the homeowners' help, we started driving again and I saw what looked like hills. They stuck out like the proverbial on such a dead flat escarpment, dotted only by shrubs.

'That'll be them,' said Stevo. There were piles of massive brown rocks, each as big as a living room, looking like a tip truck had just dumped them in the middle of nowhere.

And there was reptilian life in them thar hills. Bulky skinks no longer than a ruler, including Cunningham's (similar to the blue-tongue lizard that you find in suburbia) and the less common Hosmer's. When Hosmer's skinks scamper into crevices, they point their spiky tails and inflate their backward-facing body scales so if you try to pull them out, they wedge in tighter. And spike you.

The heat was getting to me as we tried to extract those skinks. We never followed the slip-slop-slap sun protection mantra. Stevo and I were usually hatless, shirtless, wearing footy shorts or Stubbies and occasionally sneakers. Unfortunately the photos don't lie. We got sunburnt again and again but in those days no one worried much about skin cancer. The bad habits were leftover from our normal routines back on the Sunshine Coast. We'd work outdoors all day, all seasons, from my morning bricklaying job until my last surf on dusk, and only wear dabs of zinc to protect our noses and bottom lips.

With sweaty relief I jumped a couple of metres off a rock into a shadowed cave and landed on a sandy bottom. Something heavy scurried around in there and I froze. So did it.

As my eyes adjusted I saw, only metres from me, a perentie. I'd experienced several wildlife adventures, but I'd never put myself in harm's way like this.

Stevo had only just been describing how perenties had heaps of backward-curved teeth to attack wallabies and feed on carrion. This monster had a head on him like an Alsatian dog and he was raised up on his back legs and tail.

On the ground were wallaby bones and skull fragments. I was in a perentie prey graveyard. Holy shit, what now?

'Stevo. Stevo!' I stage-whispered, not wanting to startle this thing further. The only way out was where I'd come in. I wasn't game to move.

'Stevo! Stevo!' I finally yelled. I could hear him laughing as he waltzed over to see what my problem was. Then he looked into the cave.

'Just stay still,' he said earnestly. 'Do exactly as I tell you.'

No problem there. After years of knocking around with Stevo, I respected every command he gave. He had a gift.

'Fris, move over to your left and give him a way out.'

As I did, Stevo shifted from the entrance. Whooshka! The perentie flicked his tail a couple of times and legged it, leaving dust in his wake. Stevo the diehard photographer immediately jumped down and started taking photos of all the bones, reassuring me the lizard had been as frightened as me. Maybe.

*

So what do two beach blokes do in the hottest part of the day out west? Find the nearest pub of course. Cold beer was an attraction but meeting the bushies was a necessity. You can't beat local knowledge.

At the Hamilton Hotel, north-east of Bedourie, we avoided the busload of backpackers having a feed en route to Mt Isa and Stevo went straight up to a weatherbeaten old guy. This small bloke with sparse grey hair was drinking seven-ounce (200 millilitre) glasses of straight rum.

'Mate, we're looking for this waterhole,' Stevo said.

Years later, we would still have fits of laughter imitating the cranky reply.

'Whaddya wanna know that for?' the ageing Ocker drawled. 'The last person who wanted to know that blew the hole.'

Stevo was dumbfounded. What the…?

'They blew the hole. So I'm not telling where it is. Whaddya wanna go there for?'

We figured out that someone had put dynamite in this treasured waterhole so all the fish floated to the surface for easy pickings. Stevo set him straight and that arvo we found it, pitched our tent and sat on the bank with some Bundy Rum and XXXX beer. Bob had recommended this as a camping spot with plenty of wildlife and close to where we were chasing Fierce snakes and Spencer's monitors.

In this remote area of central Queensland, everything relies on water. If animals can't find sufficient water every day, they die. So every morning at dawn and every late afternoon, we knew we'd find animals drinking.

The birdlife at this waterhole was riveting. Medium-sized birds of prey such as Black kites and Whistling kites lazily flapped their wings, searching for small mammals or fish. Noisy corellas, or white cockatoos, gathered in flocks in the trees. And it seemed incongruous to see so many budgerigars, more familiar to me as caged pets. These wild budgies were green with yellow faces and blue tails. Apparently the multicoloured domestic pets are interbred.

We dropped in a handline and I casually said, 'Wouldn't it be great to see one of those eagles (the term I used before I learnt they were actually native kites) swoop down and take something off the water?'

Stevo nodded. 'Yeah. Great to get footage of it.'

I kid you not. We were sitting maybe a metre apart when plop! Halfway between us drops a budgie, stone motherless dead, out of a tree. It was like God went, 'There you go, Stevo.'

Bizarre things just happened when you hung around Steve Irwin.

'Beauty!' we said, and threw the corpse into the drink. Within seconds a whistling kite flew down and plucked it off the water with a splash. And yes, Stevo got the incredible shot on camera.

Flying Kite: further proof of the Irwin knack, Stevo captures this amazing shot of a Kite swooping down to collect a dead budgie we'd just thrown in the Hamilton River, central western Queensland.

The next morning we woke at first light. The horizon was already disappearing into heat haze. We had only driven a few kilometres, back on to the road along the blacksoil flats, when I pointed out a beautiful snake shimmering like a piece of glass on my side of the road.

Stevo bolted from the truck. I put the handbrake on this time. Whack! He grabbed the snake by the tail and saw a second one. He ordered me to get the camera and when I turned back there he was, astride deep cracks in the clay earth, grinning as he wielded a Fierce snake in each hand.

One bite from either reptile and it would have been all over for Stevo. We were so far from help. He wasn't fazed. In fact, he tried to spread the joy. 'Do you wanna come and catch some, Fris?'

'Nah I'm right. I'm fine. You're an idiot!' I laughed.

The trip continued in the same exciting vein and we ended up with a few Spencer's monitors and Western brown snakes (again, I stayed behind the camera). We got top photos of small, insect-eating Central netted dragons which run around so much they only live two or three years in the wild (see page iv).

When we returned to the park, we faced a depressing learning curve with the Spencer's. Both died despite our nurturing. Although we couldn't afford to get autopsies done, with Bob's help we worked out their deaths were due to the breakdown of their immune systems.

When we determined that the probable cause was a combination of parasites from the roadkill already in their stomachs and stress from captivity, we resolved to never replace them.

To me, every trip with Stevo was like being at school—the educational process and PhysEd—not the boring rules and strict teachers that made me quit in Year 10. Whenever we got back in the truck, I'd fire questions at him. 'What do they feed on? What's the go with their behaviour?'

His handling techniques were always one step ahead of the animal. With snake-catching, for example, he ignored the common practice of using forked sticks. Instead he would choose a big stick with lots of leaves and twigs. I soon saw why. The snake would feel more at ease weaving in and out of the branches, which also provided an extra barrier if it did decide to strike.

These adventures were so much more than holiday snaps. We rarely wondered what everyone was doing back home, who might be partying at the pub while we were sleeping under the stars. We didn't really give a damn because we were in a better place.

Dogs accompanied us on most trips. Stevo and I loved our pets like brothers. His devotion to the two faithful canine companions he owned during his life is now immortalised in a bronze statue at Australia Zoo of his family with Sui, Stevo's second dog.

But first came Chilli, the Staffordshire terrier who never let her master out of her sight. I was there when Stevo adopted her—and in doing so saved her life—and I was there a year or so later when he saved my injured Staffie, Rhino. Ol' Stevo had a huge heart and I will never forget what I saw.

Chapter 5

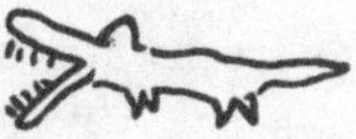

Finding Chilli dog. Paddle fast, it's closing in. Jaws in the river. Jump for it! The dangers of education.

In our late teens/early 20s Stevo and I did several trips to the Lockhart River area on the east coast of Cape York Peninsula. One of the most northern villages in Queensland, Lockhart River is more than 2000 kilometres (1200 miles) from the Sunshine Coast and adjoins the stunning Iron Range National Park. The state government now considers it 'of international significance' as the largest lowland rainforest left in Australia, a haven for birdlife surrounded by eucalypt and paperbark forest.

You have to go in the dry season, from mid-year to about November, to avoid monsoon rainfall and 45-degree (113 Fahrenheit) heat. There are saltwater crocodiles, sharks, snakes, stonefish, stinging jellyfish and even stinging trees. None of these bothered Stevo at work or play. I was more wary.

We arrived at the first crossing of the Claudie River late at night after 27 hours behind the wheel. We rolled out our swags beside the truck and managed to build a small fire despite the difficulties in a moist rainforest.

Noticing our stuff was right on the edge of a crystal-clear stream, I looked to Stevo for reassurance that there were no crocodiles. On inspection of the water with our trusty Dolphin torches, the only red eye shines were from large freshwater shrimp the length of two-litre milk bottles.

Stevo suggested we catch a few to ease our rumbling stomachs. Have you ever tried to catch shrimp with your bare hands? It's useless. They flick backwards really quickly and are like lightning in the water. Rather than find a suitable net, my mate showed me an old bush technique.

He split the end of a green stick which was pliable enough to act like tongs. Then he stuck a match in the tines to keep them apart until the stick was in position above one of the submerged crustaceans. In the blink of an eye, Stevo jammed the stick on to the shrimp. As the match dislodged, the tongs sprang back together. It was well and truly caught.

After we had boiled some on the fire and washed them down with a couple of beers, sleep came rapidly.

We awoke to a horrible stench, sickly sweet and overpowering. Was it rotting fruit? A rainforest tree in bloom?

No, daylight revealed we had camped directly under a flying fox colony. The big bats' droppings were on everything. Including us.

We drove across to Chili Beach, right on the edge of the blue-green Coral Sea. Forget those pictures of Fiji or the Maldives, this was our perfect oasis. White sand, giant swaying palm trees, coral reefs extending out to a small tropical island—and our dirty red four-wheel-drive with a dinghy on the back. At high tide we dived around the mangroves and reefs for crayfish and Mangrove jack. Delicious eating. As someone prone to impatience, I certainly preferred spearfishing to the ol' rod and reel. (It also meant avoiding 'jack attacks', when these native fighting fish snap off your lure.)

A Staffie pup turned up at our campsite so we fed her. We asked the few local hippies and alternatives who owned her. No one knew. She kept hanging around and was back the following day.

At one point this hobo rocked up with a flagon of red wine and slobbered to us, 'Do you want some of this?'

We laughed. 'No mate, you're right, we're fine.'

He started telling us about working on a trawler when the dog came over. He kicked it. Stevo gave him a serve, he wasn't going to put up with that.

When we were ready to leave, the plucky pup started jogging behind my red HiLux. Stevo looked back and announced, 'I'm taking this dog'. She was only getting abused up there, not fed. We sat there and picked dozens of scrub ticks off her and threw them on the campfire.

So that's how Chilli got her name. She was only small and she was the cutest thing and they became so, so close.

From then on Stevo never went anywhere without her. If he was going out to a party at night back on the Coast he'd say, 'Chilli, jump!' and she'd be in the car. If we went pigging in the bush, she'd be in the thick of the action.

Man's best friends: Stevo's beloved new puppy Sui befriends Tony and Melinda's Staffie Rhino in 1988. Rhino was the dog kicked by a cow and revived by Stevo.

*

We were right into pig shooting in those days. It might seem odd for such animal lovers but we knew feral pigs, and feral cats for that matter, were destroying native wildlife. To understand conservation properly you often had to accept the cruelty of the food chain and survival of the fittest in the wild. Plus pigs made great bait when we started trapping giant crocs.

Days before we got Chilli and after stocking up on fuel at Lockhart River, we were en route to another crossing of the Claudie River when Stevo and I drove past a turkey's nest dam. His eyes lit up.

We saw impressive trotter tracks around it and reckoned, 'Oh yeah, this is us. There's a huge boar working in this area.'

A turkey's nest dam is a small, circular dam built above ground using earth from around the site for the walls. Usually fed by groundwater bores, this one was probably only 20 metres (65 feet) across.

We were nutters, granted. We ran fishing line around the dam and on the end tied empty beer cans. Any pig that walked into that waterhole would hit the fishing line, rattle the cans and alert us.

Many hours and beers later it was dark and I was almost asleep. Stevo, of course, was not. He woke me with a loud whisper, 'There's a big pig!'

The mosquitoes were like the plague but we couldn't spray Aerogard or swat them. We couldn't make any noise.

We had connected a spotlight to a mobile battery and I had the pump action shotgun ready.

Shotguns aren't designed for shooting pigs but we had developed a way. When standing in the back of the truck to chase pigs across open plains, you'd load up with solid bullets. When you shot it at night the rifle threw out a flame that you could see in the spotlight and headlights of the car. A 12 gauge shotgun cartridge contains small pellets which you could also see hitting the dust around the pig. That would be your guide for the second and fatal shot using a lead solid.

Suddenly Stevo hit the spotlight. I reacted with the shotgun. Stevo had a .308 Valmet and he let go a few shots as well. The solid from my gun landed behind the pig's front leg, killing it instantly. Immature as we were, we spent ages boasting of our success before returning at daylight to get trophy photos.

*

Stevo and I honed our pigging skills on subsequent trips with Chilli and my older dog Rhino. Our dogs also became good mates, in the bush and on home turf.

Back then Staffies weren't popular on the Sunshine Coast for some reason, so people enjoyed watching these two knock around together. Chilli couldn't fathom Rhino's love-hate relationship with the pandanus trees in front of the rock groyne at Kings Beach, however.

We'd drive down there to go surfing and I'd put a branch inside the bullbar or towbar of the car. Rhino would leap up, grab it and simply hang there for half an hour. Unfortunately he would then rip apart the pandanus roots.

Chilli ignored such nonsense. Her duty always called: her master. And he was usually slamming down the crest of a crazy wave, dreaming up his next mad challenge.

*

For much of the 1980s the Irwins were contracted by the Queensland National Parks and Wildlife Service to capture and remove crocodiles that were endangering people or property in the state's north. As a volunteer I happily tagged along for many of the rides.

By the late '80s, the East Coast Crocodile Management Program was a very formal business with heaps of paperwork. At the time it was annoying, but in June 2008—as I wrote this chapter—Bob was amazed and touched to receive framed originals of these $10 permits, signed by Stevo, found during a government office cleanout at Ingham.

The permits, from 1989 and 1990, had allowed us to relocate saltwater (also known as estuarine) crocodiles from waterways between Crystal Creek and the Burdekin River, near Ingham, to the Beerwah park.

Millions of visitors can still see some of these crocs at the zoo—

including the 600-kilogram (1300-pound) Agro and Acco, a 4.5-metre (15-foot) gargantuan Stevo caught by himself. Acco now weighs 1000 kilograms (2200 pounds) and is possibly more than 70 years old.

After I discovered what those expeditions entailed, I realised the paperwork was the least of our worries.

I met my first aggressive north Queensland crocodile by accident. It was 1983 and Stevo and I were on an expedition to catch Mangrove monitors near Weipa, a mining town on the western side of Cape York Peninsula facing the Gulf of Carpentaria.

Stevo's croc knowledge was still expanding. I hadn't had much to do with them yet in the wild. What I learnt that day has stuck with me throughout my own reptile-handling career.

We reached Andoom River, north of Weipa's enormous bauxite mine, in search of the mangrove monitors. These shy, water-loving lizards are dark-scaled with yellow spots and up to a metre long. The head is a fair bit smaller than the neck, but it can drop its lower jaw to devour sizeable prey.

We were recovering from a dodgy encounter of the human kind the previous night at a local pub. A guy had been mouthing off about killing crocs and we ended up in a bit of trouble. By trouble, I mean the watchhouse.

This local crocodile poacher, who had hunted the animals before they became protected, started bragging about how he used to catch juveniles and kill them for taxidermy. He reckoned he had worked with a legendary croc hunter known as German Jack. (Mind you German Jack was only a legend to those who didn't understand crocs.)

When this poacher explained how he did the killings, Stevo sprayed him with choice words. Then it was on. Punches flew between the three of us until a copper made us spend most of an uncomfortable night at the station.

*

Chapter 5

That morning was serene and sunny so Stevo and I put our little flatbottom punt in the river beside the Andoom bridge. We headed downstream on this huge river—about 200 metres (660 feet) wide with steep banks lined by mangroves. No other boats were around. In those days Weipa was remote, populated mostly by mineworkers and Aboriginal communities.

The poor punt had a tough job hauling two blokes' 150-kilogram (330 pound) combined weight with only a three or four horsepower Tohatsu outboard motor freeboarding by just 150 millimetres (6 inches). We cruised down to the mouth, scouring the banks for these particular lizards that live in mud so deep you can sink up to your waist. The sides of the boat were not high. Our bodies seemed very close to the ripples.

The wind blew just enough that you could hear the punt reverberating on the water.

As we began the return journey we heard puh-puh-puh-puhhhhh. It was out of fuel.

'Well, fill it up,' Stevo said.

'Did you get fuel?' I asked.

'Nup. Did you?'

Hmm. Our silly little paddles came into play. I was sitting on the second front seat. Stevo was steering at the back. I paddled silently. To our right, sliding gracefully off the bank into the river, was a 4-metre (13-foot) crocodile. Guess how long our punt was? Yep, 13 foot.

The saltie stayed on the surface, headed straight towards the boat then dropped out of sight.

'He was nice 'eh?' said Stevo.

As we kept paddling I realised the tide was coming in with us, so I had a rest and looked behind. About 50 metres (160 feet), maybe less, behind the boat was this crocodile. He was following the boat. And he was closing in.

'Stevo, that croc's following us.'

'Yeah, has been all the time.'

'It's pretty big.'

'Yeah, just keep paddling Fris.' He suggested that if I felt scared I should bang the wooden paddle on the aluminium side.

Bang! Bang! Bang!

The animal got within 15 metres (50 feet) of the boat, close enough for us to see his eyes and the osteoderms, or bony plates, behind his head. I knew a croc this size could launch an attack very fast over this distance. I knew if that great head came up next to the boat his eyes would meet mine at the same level.

Was I packing death? Absolutely.

The croc kept arching his tail and rising out of the water, showing himself. Stevo told me he was displaying his size. 'He's saying, "If you wanna muck around with me, this is how big I am."'

Ahead I could see the bridge where we'd parked the truck. Naïvely, I asked if we could just sweep into shore and escape. The answer was swift.

'If you go to that bank, that crocodile will hit you right now.'

The riverbanks offered no sanctuary—crocs love to grab prey when surrounded by slippery, sucking mud.

So I kept paddling and banging. I never asked if the noise was meant to ward off the croc or make me feel better.

Our salvation came when we reached a certain point past the bridge and the croc stopped, turned sideways and puffed his body up and down, until we could hardly see him in the distance.

'That's the end of his territory,' explained Stevo. 'He didn't want to eat us. All he wanted was us out of his territory.'

You'd think that little episode would have put me off. Funny thing was, it gave me an adrenalin rush I couldn't wait to repeat. As soon as possible. With my expert buddy close by.

It sparked my lifelong fascination with these much-maligned predators, offering an insight into croc behaviour when under threat. We put this knowledge to excellent use as we became more game in the future.

*

Over a few summers until the mid '80s we did several trips to Cattle Creek. I was barely 20 but Stevo decided I was ready to jump and trap wild crocs. Luckily we started off small.

Cattle Creek is a seasonal wetlands/farming area about 30 kilometres (18 miles) south of Ingham, halfway between Townsville and Cairns on the tropical north-east coast. Salt and freshwater crocs are more visible in summer because they're more active—eating and breeding—but this also makes them territorial, protective and cranky. In an annoying coincidence, it's also the hottest and wettest season. Roads and tracks get cut off faster than a truck can accelerate.

Concentrating and sweating, we were perched in the boat along a narrow tributary called Waterfall Creek when Stevo suddenly said, 'Get up the front.'

I moved.

He continued. 'When we get close enough, leap off and grab that croc down the base of the neck and hang on. Place the tail between your legs and just hang on to 'er.'

The water was fairly shallow—low tide is best for croc spotting—but I must have looked dubiously at my selected animal.

Stevo said, 'She's only two or three foot (under a metre). You'll be right, Fris.'

I jumped out and instinctively grabbed it as I landed with a great deal of splashing. The bugger then twisted—they're strong for their size—but I held on. Its skin was smoother than you'd expect, even those knobbly rows of scutes down the back and tail, but I hung on for dear life.

Success. I won a croc and my self-confidence. We got the animal in the boat, blindfolded it and tied it comfortably. Back at camp we prepared it for processing—and I don't mean eating or skinning.

This croc was caught and relocated as part of the East Coast Crocodile Management Program after complaints from landowners. I learnt that the program kicked into gear if a croc was threatening a person or their livelihood, for example fishermen or farmers or livestock. First we would try to educate residents, help them understand crocs and hopefully live safely with them. Stevo even tried to convince people of his theory that a croc's shock at being trapped could often be enough deterrent for it to stay far away from human interaction (such as fearing the sound of a boat's motor).

But back then, awareness was so low and fear so high that many people just didn't want to hear it. So if that process failed, the program focused on removal and relocation.

Of course, it was a wonderful boon for Bob's fledgling zoo despite the dangers. I became proud of the fact that we sourced all of the sub-adult crocs in the park's burgeoning enclosures using this jumping technique. Crocs can live longer than a century so many of them are still living in luxury at Australia Zoo.

Over the next few years I would discover that leaping on bigger ones, 1.5 metres (5 foot) and over, meant going into deep water. And that meant trying to control the awkward writhing without sinking. Not so squeezy.

Chapter 6

Trawling for crocs. How Stevo brought Rhino back from the dead. No sleep 'til…

On another eerie late afternoon at Waterfall Creek, Stevo and I were carefully preparing for night croc-trapping. Spotties and batteries were tested and re-tested. I don't know how we fit all the necessary equipment in a 14-foot (4-metre) tinnie.

The process steadied my nerves until we untied from the bank and softly motored away amid ominous darkness and overhanging mangroves.

There was no moon. The boat was painted flat black to stop reflection from our spotlight blinding us. Stevo was experimenting with different coloured reflectors on the spotlights to get closer to the crocs, especially the old, cunning ones who had lived through the rampant shooting era. (Crocs became legally protected in Queensland in 1974.) Sceptics in the industry ridiculed his technique at the time, but it has now been adopted by Queensland Parks and Wildlife for crocodile surveys.

It was low tide and eerie. All I could smell was outboard fuel.

Suddenly all these prawns were jumping out of the water into the boat. Damn! Prawns everywhere. I was up the front with the spotlight and pretty jumpy myself as I glanced at the big trawler net in the middle of the boat.

We continued heading for Cattle Creek. 'Heads!' I yelled as I pulled us around low-slung branches. Leaping mullet hit the sides. I guess I'd expected silence, not this continual splashing.

Something soft hit my face. Ugh, huge fat moth. Better that than a giant spider, though. I really hated bush spiders. Whoops, spoke too soon. Our faces were enveloped by enormous, wire-like cobwebs. The sticky strands gave me the creeps.

We spotted red eye shines. A croc? No, they were the eyes of insectivorous birds known as nightjars.

We saw one, two, three sets of birds' eyes on the riverbanks. Snap! Crocodile peepers. 'There's one Stevo!'

We crept closer. Checked him out. Nup, not right. Continued cruising. Another croc pulled under the water.

'That'll be a bigger animal,' Stevo noted. He seemed to know every bend and how every croc related to a particular territory. I remembered Bob teaching us these things in the old shed, pointing to maps and drawings on the ping pong table.

Prawns plopped into the boat. Moths whirred by. It felt like every bug in Australia was caught in my shirt, biting skin. Turning the spotlight on another section of bank, I said, 'There's a fox up there.'

'What? Where?' Stevo said, trying to grab the spotlight, which was heating my hand. 'Switch the light off.'

'What's wrong?' I said.

'That's a croc on that bank.'

'Oh. No worries.' I tried to sound cool about it.

He turned the boat and took us back past it. He clicked on the spotlight, confirmed the croc and clicked it off immediately. Because of the tide, the steep bank was about 2 metres (6.5 feet) high. Bringing us in close, he said, 'Tie off the front of the net there. We're gonna catch this one.'

'You're kiddin' aren't ya?' I said. 'How big is he?'

'About 9 or 10 foot (3 metres).' Close to the size of our dinghy.

In almost total darkness, we swung the net in an arc in the water below the animal, reversing the boat to get it in place. Flick. Spotlight on. The croc's head had shifted. All I could see was this long jagged jaw above me, sticking over the side of the bank.

Full-on fear. In hindsight, I realised the croc only had one place to go. Straight into the water.

Suddenly it launched off the bank, right in front of the boat. As it hit, its body skimmed on the surface and slid across the floats of the net, into deeper water.

'Oh! We bloody missed it,' said Stevo.

I silently thanked God and snapped, 'What would you have done if it landed in the boat?'

Poker-faced, he said, 'We would have had it then. Beautiful.'

And that was my trial run. The start of real-life night terrors.

The next day we returned to the scene and Stevo discovered the croc had been sitting on a wallaby track, waiting for a feed to come along. He processed the data, eyes narrowing with concentration, and formed a new plan.

*

Bob had taught his son the benefits of bag traps instead of the steel cages with drop-down gates commonly used by other zoos and croc farms. The Irwins wanted to prevent crocs injuring themselves from banging their heads against steel or smashing their snouts trying to escape. In the wild we'd seen cornered crocs hurl back their heads so violently they sheared off mangroves as thick as a stubby. Imagine the suffering if they tried that on inflexible steel instead of natural timber.

Years later when I worked for the government I was forced to use gate traps because of workplace health and safety rules. They were hard on the animals and crocs would end up with mangled snouts and broken teeth. With the Irwins, animal welfare always came first. Irwin traps, made of thick trawler mesh, had a big opening that tapered like a sock. Stevo had spent long nights in his shed at the park modifying them until he had it down to a fine art.

He had the trigger mechanism set exactly so that once the croc had been lured inside the bag, the counterweight would drop and pull the drawstring tight. Like a slipknot. The bag then closed around the reptile, protecting it. He even had different types of mesh, which fishermen recognised by the black, blue or green colours, for different circumstances.

So I followed Stevo's lead. Once we identified a croc's slide, we'd hop out of the boat into warm, disgusting, thigh-deep mud. Sometimes we wore overalls, but often just long-sleeved shirts and shorts. You'd sink into it, fall forward, end up on your guts, and pull yourself further up the bank. Then you'd have to go back to the boat for the pig, probably shot the previous day, probably crawling with maggots. (Later you discovered the futility of trying to scrape off the mud—it sticks to your skin and leg hairs like super glue.)

We'd dig up a heap of this mud to fill a hessian bag, tie it off with rope, then haul it high into tree branches to act as the counterweight. When filled with wet mud these old fertiliser bags weighed up to 70 kilograms (154 pounds). Sometimes two were required. Yet Stevo would yank 'em up into the trees, spurred only by swearing and sweating. If I hadn't seen his agility and brute strength myself, I would never have believed he also did this solo, over and over, for months on end, in this unforgiving scrub with only his dog for company.

We attached the rope to the front of the trap and set the bait of bloody pig carcass. Around the back we set up the trigger mechanism, basically a piece of steel with a couple of nails attached to the rope. Then we waited.

And waited. Every morning for a week we checked the traps. Empty.

Squelching around in 35 to 40-degree heat (95-104 Fahrenheit), we slapped at biting mosquitoes, sandflies and green ants. I was ready to give up but Stevo knew we would succeed if we used patience and skill.

He honed a personal technique to make crocs feel secure when approaching a trap site. These primitive animals had great survival instincts and the smell of humans and manmade structures in their area was often enough to deter them.

Stevo jammed a stick in the mud just above the high tide mark and attached to it a piece of juicy pig the size of a man's fist. He intended this 'leading bait' to entice the croc into the trap's entrance nearby. He spent ages stacking sticks and brush around the sides of the trap as a barricade to prevent crocs, boars or goannas from sneaking around the side to get the bait while keeping their freedom.

One morning the leading bait was gone.

The next morning we returned, adrenalin pumping.

Snatched! Finally, we had it. Her. She was about 2.5-metres (8-feet) long, as big as the ladies grow. I should have known Stevo wouldn't give up. He named her Molly.

Molly was probably the biggest croc I'd caught so far, and she took some getting into the boat. We had to tip the boat on its side on the edge of shallow water, wedging sticks against it, and push/pull her into it. She was heavy and stubborn. It still amazes me that Stevo performed these sorts of manoeuvres in the wild by himself.

We took Molly back to the park. Another so-called rogue saved from a landowner's rifle thanks to the East Coast Crocodile Management Program. She'd been targeted because her creek backed on to farmland.

I don't think Stevo ever quite got over the guilt of yanking these magnificent creatures from the domains they'd inhabited for decades. I remember the admiration in my mate's eyes on the few occasions we spotted Acco's eye shine in his creek. That monster was so smart. We'd see his red eye shine, blink, and he'd disappear. Stevo would roll a smoke, drift with the tide, try to bluff him with silence. Nothing.

Stevo ended up catching Acco by himself. No one could comprehend how he got the croc in the boat, considering a backhoe was needed to lift Acco back on to land. Stevo said he knew he had to do it, because sooner or later the croc would make a mistake and get shot by a worried resident. But in fulfilling this 'duty of care' to humans, Stevo knew he was wrecking the croc family structure in that environment.

I still pinch myself about getting such rare chances to learn about Aussie wildlife directly from the Irwins. Many people read books to learn, but for me, the best method was hands-on. I became very serious about passing on this passion and knowledge throughout my own career, later putting the techniques to good use at Hartley's Creek Crocodile Farm and returning to the zoo with tricks of my own.

*

We were getting ready to wrap up a Cattle Creek conquest when we got an urgent call from Bob in Beerwah. Another farmer up our way had complained to the state department about a rogue croc on his property, in this sugar-growing and beef cattle region.

The department asked the Irwins to investigate. Apparently the croc had been chewing up a float on the foot valve of a pump in the river. The farmer intended to kill it.

The farmer took us down to this chewed suction pump and Stevo found scratch marks on the riverbank indicating a reptile between 2.5 and 3 metres (8-10 feet). He started the gradual process of assessing the crocodilian's personality and habits before setting leading baits to gain its confidence before the trap.

This technique of treating crocodiles individually made Stevo stand out from other trappers. It reflected his passion and love for the creatures but, damn, it could be slow going.

When we finally caught the wary female, she was a beauty. We took great pleasure in saving her life and later installing her in the privileged ponds at the park.

In the bush on the way back we spotted wild pigs mixed in with cows. Before we had time to wonder if our pork bait stocks needed replenishing, my dog Rhino leapt from the back of the truck and took off after a pig. He missed it and instead grabbed a cow by the tail.

This cow started flogging him, flinging his body around. I was shouting for him to come. Finally he let go, but as he landed on the ground the cow kicked. Its powerful hoof hit Rhino fair in the chest.

Panic. It looked real bad, even from that distance. I bolted towards my poor dog. Stevo wasn't far behind.

Breathing heavily, we came to a standstill above the motionless barrel of fur.

Rhino was dead. Bang. Out. His eyes had rolled back; he was bleeding from his ears and his nose.

I stared in shock. How could such a tough dog be killed so quickly? The tears started as I leant over him. 'He's gone Stevo, he's gone,' I said.

'No he's not, Fris,' he said quietly.

I couldn't comprehend Stevo's words as he crouched down beside Rhino. Surely he could see what I saw.

But Stevo's actions were clear. He cupped his hands around Rhino's mouth and nose and took a deep breath.

Then he started blowing. And Rhino started moving.

The bloody dog came back!

Within minutes, Rhino was gasping for breath. It was amazing. My mate did mouth-to-mouth on my dog. We both sat down and tried to keep Rhino cool and immobile. Eventually he got up and walked, a bit sore and tender by the look of him. Stevo wedged him in the front of the truck for the ride back to our campsite.

I said, 'No, he'll be right in the back. Plenty of room for him to lie down.'

Of course Rhino decided to stand up in the back just as we came to a patch of mud. Stevo had to gun it and we hit a bump in the middle. My dog flew off.

I whipped my head around and saw him disappear into the murk.

'Rhino's out!' I yelled. Stevo cursed and stamped on the brake. As we pulled up, Rhino was dragging himself out, soaked.

This time I listened to Stevo, who sat Rhino gingerly in the front, mud everywhere.

Back at camp we washed his battered body and he didn't move for three days. But he recovered. Staffies are as tough as trucks.

I would never forget that canine kiss of life.

*

Stevo operated totally on adrenalin. He enjoyed a drink and a cigarette with us back when smoking was common, but his natural high was far more powerful, especially when animal welfare was at stake. For example, we commonly did the drive from the Sunshine Coast to Iron Range in just a day. Stevo drove the lot, only breaking for fuel. He knew time could mean life or death for a reptile at risk in its habitat.

I and occasionally Mick, and later young Wes Mannion (now Australia Zoo director) were the only friends who went away with Stevo on these trips because no one else could keep up. He operated on no sleep. If you weren't in that same frame of mind, with that same capacity, you got left behind.

Stevo would get tunnel vision: 'I must do this now.' His trade was diesel-fitting and he was always tinkering. If he set himself a mission at the park, he wouldn't leave until that job was finished. Night or day, it didn't matter. It was amazing.

Of course he always took it six steps too far. When I was about 17, a few of Stevo's mates got worried calls from his mum Lyn at the park. She told us Stevo had been bitten by a baby Collett's snake, a member of the venomous black snake family, while helping it out of its egg. She said he was very sick but of course was refusing to get medical help. She wanted us to round him up.

When a couple of us mates got to the park, we saw Stevo was crook all right—but still working. We couldn't believe he was raking and cleaning while intermittently vomiting as a deathly sweat poured off him.

I presumed he didn't want to admit he'd made a mistake. But it could have killed him. Bob must have been away or he would have clipped him round the ear and told him to pull his head in, and go see a doctor.

As Mr Invincible gradually improved despite the lack of medical assistance, he explained that he'd been helping the baby Collett's out of its egg in the breeding shed when whack! The critter fanged him on the thumb.

'No dramas, I knew it might affect me a bit,' Stevo summarised. He did know a lot about toxicity, but it was still bloody stupid.

*

During all those years of mateship, as we grew from teenagers into men, I watched Stevo adopt many of his parents' characteristics. But he also frequently broke out of the no-nonsense exterior, playing silly buggers or showing raw emotion. These moments could be unexpected but, as you will see, they brought us closer.

Chapter 7

They're not crocodile tears. Seeking the Holy Grail. Stevo's sexual desert. Going for gold on the Goldie. Flirting with fate.

Stevo had brutally strong feelings and, positive or negative, he let them fly. He broke down crying on many occasions. I guess if you didn't know him you might have been surprised but, to me, it was just Stevo being honest. Despite my macho nature, I never considered this a sign of weakness.

I remember walking through the park with him towards the turtle enclosure early one morning. We found 11 dead Saw-shell and Long-neck turtles. Their scattered, immobile carapaces formed a pitiful picture.

A dirty rotten canetoad had got inside. The turtles had eaten the poisonous canetoad eggs, which killed them. Stevo was in tears, his shoulders shaking.

He had the same reaction years later after the death of our 22-foot (6.5-metre) python—the biggest captive snake in Queensland. Its body is now on display in a glass case near the food court at Australia Zoo.

And his devastation was heartbreaking when Chilli dog died in

1988. The loyal Staffie was accidentally shot by a farmer's son at Cattle Creek while they were hunting for croc food.

Stevo buried her nearby, just up from Waterfall Creek, at a favourite campsite built by Bob. They named it Camp Chilli. Bob has now taken the name for his own wildlife sanctuary near Kingaroy.

When Stevo returned to the Sunshine Coast he was inconsolable. He just closed up.

'Mate, you can get another dog,' I said. He just shook his head.

We were so relieved about six months later when he turned up at my place at Currimundi with a furry brown bundle of energy. This new Staffie cross was just as smart and courageous as Chilli and acted like a little sister to my dog Rhino. But what to name her? Stevo knew she was going to be a pigger in remote terrain so he wanted vowels that echoed for kilometres. We discussed how difficult it could be calling my dog. 'Rhino' doesn't travel well through the bush. 'Suuuuu-eeeeee' certainly did, given that it sounded so similar to that traditional Aussie call, 'cooee'. So he smiled and named her Sui.

*

Chris White remembers the worst physical pain he ever saw Steve in was when he did his knee at footy during high school. Whitey also recalls Steve's occasional jealousy over girls, and how much he hated animal deaths. But the worst emotional reaction Chris saw was when Lyn died.

'Steve and I often shot the breeze on his mobile but this time he was a total mess,' Chris recalls. 'Many tears. It rattled him because he was really close to his mum, they shared the same birthday.'

Di Schwenke also recalls Steve's emotional extremes, from Indiana Jones to ol' softie.

'He was as tough as nails,' she says, 'but he had a sensitive side. He wasn't a macho or gruff person and he could be a real gentleman to the ladies. And he adored his parents. Sometimes if he was having issues with his folks, the normal growing-up stuff, he'd just take off—go troppo on his own to think it through. Other times he'd come visit us at Currimundi and just cry. He was pretty passionate, like his mum.'

Di remembers Steve as a smart cookie, 'always searching for the Holy Grail', finding his answers in nature and conservation. 'You could sense in him that he lived for every minute. That's why he didn't like sleeping much.'

*

Stevo's empathy for animals was the essence of his personality years before the publicity machine dreamed up the Crocodile Hunter. This was a moniker made for television documentaries around the time he turned 30.

I copped a fair ribbing because of my link to 'that Crikey dickhead'. I took it on the chin but would retort with, 'Would you take any notice of his message if he was just standing there speaking normally?' It pissed me off to hear strangers dismiss Steve Irwin as fake because of cynicism surrounding the hype.

The Steve I knew was pretty much the same Steve we all saw later on TV because saving animals always was the driving force in his life. (And I have to admit, he did say 'crikey' a lot.) I saw how much of Lyn's influence rubbed off on him. He would pull up on the side of the road if a female wallaby had been hit by a car so he could check her pouch for a joey. He went out in his own time to remove snakes from people's houses so the snakes wouldn't be killed.

If a tree had to be cut down, he checked it for sugar gliders and either stopped the chop or safely removed the cute little possums and raised them. One day we found a large turtle stranded on Rainbow Beach. The surf was really rough and it was buggered. Stevo worried it wouldn't get back out. He gripped its heavy shell and swam it out himself, past the churning breakers, and let it go in calmer seas.

But he saved his greatest love for crocodiles. 'She's a darling, Fris,' is how he described a scaly, spiky female saltie named Joan Collins that had once bitten him on the calf. Stevo talked about his crocs like they were his girlfriends.

The affection was a little unnerving, especially when his relationships with human girlfriends were far more unstable. They didn't last more than a few months. As he told his old man frequently, 'I live in a sexual desert.'

Sandy-haired, sensitive Stevo was forward with the ladies and could be a heartbreaker, but his luck always ran out. The pretty girls he wooed were definitely drawn to his charisma, but in the end they chose normality. Sunshine Coast chicks just weren't into his interests.

He did some crazy things for love. After one girlfriend locked him out of her third-storey unit overlooking Pumicestone Passage, the human orang-utan shinnied up three balconies to beg entry. One false move and it would have been all over, red rover.

Then there was the chick he picked up at the carwash.

A dozen of us mates were driving back in our cars after the annual Stubbies Surf Classic down the Gold Coast. In this annual gathering of legends at Burleigh Heads, Peter Drouyn pioneered the man-on-man system where only two surfers competed in each heat. Named after Stubbies clothing, its 30th anniversary in 2007 reunited the likes of Tom Carroll, Rabbit Bartholomew and MR Richards.

We were all in our early 20s and in high spirits after a huge weekend on the turps, despite a dodgy start at a motel in Tugun.

We'd booked this place over the phone and it was a choice joint. When we walked in the owner gave us the drum on what we could and couldn't do. One rule was pretty normal—don't make noise after a certain time. But the other?

'All right boys,' he said, 'I don't want you cutting up me garden hose. There's hose in the freezer you can use.' We couldn't work out if he was stereotyping surfers as bong-suckers or if he was simply accustomed to that kind of clientele. When we looked down and saw our legs covered in fleas, we were outta there.

Of course we hooked up with a group of chicks, told tales. Rod declared that he was a travelling pet food salesman and I was a pro surfer's younger brother. But Stevo waited until the very end of the weekend to make his move. Waited, in fact, until we were going past a garage at Chermside in Brisbane, halfway home. He spotted a bunch of bikini babes washing cars.

Three car washes later, he'd talked one of them into coming to Margarita's that night. Wouldn't you know it, she actually turned up too.

*

So often Stevo complained to me, 'I'm not gonna find a girl in a nightclub. Where am I going to get a girl?'

It's also possible some of them objected to his warped humour. In the mid '80s Stevo and Mick did a trip to Cape York. I had bricklaying work and couldn't go. They found a way to get me back.

I was still living at Mum's at Golden Beach. So was my cousin Pete. I was pretty wild, only coming home to eat, sleep and get my washing done.

'Or he wouldn't come home at all,' recalls Pete. 'Tony hadn't been home for days when something started stinking. His mother kept her house spotless. We couldn't work out where the hell it was coming from. There was mail for Tony sitting on the kitchen bench.'

It was a small package, one of those bubblewrap postpacks. They demanded I open it as soon as I walked in. We were all heaving. I took the package out the back, ripped into it and read a note from Stevo. 'Wish you were here' or something dumb like that.

Inside? Pigs' ears. Absolutely green with decomposition. It was gross. We couldn't stop laughing. Except Mum.

*

Jibba recalls his own Gold Coast golden moment with Stevo.

'When Steve was going to TAFE college in Brisbane to be a diesel mechanic, he'd often bring good-looking birds back up the Coast to introduce to us,' Jibba says. 'We'd be impressed. "Gee, she's all right, Steve." But two weeks later, she'd be gone. We'd never know what happened. So when groups of us guys went to the Gold Coast on these surfing trips, we'd try our luck at this resort nightclub on Cavill Avenue.

'One afternoon four of us parked Steve's white Honda Accord at the top of Cavill, left the keys on top of the wheel, moved our surfboards from the roof into the car, changed into our good gear and walked straight to the bar. We gave prizes to each other for the best pick-up story. That night I was a helicopter pilot. We met four great girls and ran amok, losing each other at different points. I remember sleeping on the carpet in a hotel room and hearing Steve's voice, outside the building somewhere, yelling "Jibba? Jibba where are you?"

'In the morning a few of us were eating bacon and eggs at an outdoor cafe. Voooom! I see Steve's Honda belting past. Next minute…voooom! Back the other way. We were yelling, running down the street to catch him. Steve was either lost and looking for us or pretending he hadn't spotted us to get his kicks. We had to cut that whole trip short because we'd blown all our money in one night.'

Funnily enough, Whitey has a Gold Coast tale too.

'Growing up as mates we really had no thoughts of girlfriends. Surfing and rugby league were our life. Until we got licences. Then girls arrived on the scene. I remember going on surfing safaris down south with Steve, Mick and Jibba. We'd base ourselves at the Goldie and go wherever the surf was pumping. The four of us took out the same four girls on these trips for about six months. Probably a record for us at the time.'

*

One of the most significant turning points in Stevo's youth began in May 1984 when he and Mick went on a six-month boys' adventure overseas. They returned full of beans and spinning a flurry of yarns about wild times in Thailand.

Stevo had turned 22 on 22 February and, while he'd obviously had crazy fun, the holiday aftermath left him unsettled. He seemed uncertain of his future direction, unsure of the Holy Grail. Then, all of a sudden, he made a decision to grow up. He crystallised his commitment to the park, and crocodiles in particular. The rebel got his cause. He decided that one day he would take over from his folks.

I watched as Stevo's focus sharpened. He was already obsessive about wildlife but this newfound maturity made him even more dedicated to the park's success. His trade became a tool, his socialising secondary. The park was his domain—something he could control, something he got great satisfaction from. Bob remembers this as a major turning point, too.

Getting up at 4am and going to bed at 11pm was not unusual for Stevo. He would slave all day then sleep so lightly that one bark would send him flying into the enclosures brandishing a Dolphin torch and a .22 rifle, keeping watch for cats or foxes trying to get at zoo animals. Control freak? For sure.

However, man is not an island and poor Stevo first had to deal with another bad relationship bust-up. In fact he came close to blows with his ex's new suitor after the Thailand trip. Unfortunately I was piggy in the middle because I was friends with all of them. There's no way I'd take on Stevo, though. Even with my background, he was far too big, strong and aggressive. Sure I could box, but if he grabbed me, I knew he wouldn't let go!

It was an awkward time for our group socially. Stevo might have been the 'alpha male', but he wasn't the only one adjusting to change or forging a career while dealing with the rollercoaster of life and love. There was general turmoil over girls.

My sister Mandy started dating Chris White, who copped the nickname Dingo for being a 'baby snatcher'. She was only five years younger than him. I always had a lot of respect for Chris, however, and was stoked when they got engaged.

I was 20 and busy courting my future wife Melinda Uhlmann. Stevo complained to me. 'How come you've got one who likes to go camping? How'd an ugly bastard like you get her?' We enjoyed sharing terms of endearment.

*

Melinda was indeed a babe, a finalist in the Surf Girl competition, and she loved the outdoors. Her family had moved from Brisbane to Caloundra after spending regular weekends at their Golden Beach holiday house.

I knew Melinda's older brother Grant, who would head out with local surfers. And when the Uhlmanns became locals, Melinda's older sister dated a guy we knew who surfed Kings and Moffat. One day Grant made the mistake of bringing his little sis to the beach.

'I should give her 20 cents and tell her to ring me in a couple of years,' I told him at the old Kings Beach kiosk. (Melinda is four years younger than me.)

'You can stay away from my sister,' he replied amid much laughter and mumbling from the crew.

Melinda often sunbathed on Kings Beach. I would casually throw water bombs at her to get her attention. And I don't mean little balloons. We got empty bread bags from the shop and filled them to the brim with water. Somehow it worked. One Christmas morning she was walking back from the beach when I pulled over in my white Telstar—it had a tacho with flashing lights, pretty cool in those days—and asked if she wanted to have Christmas lunch.

She accepted. Her family was hosting Christmas dinner so she wasn't needed at home for a while. That was the beginning. Sorry Grant.

Melinda was drop-dead gorgeous with a beautiful smile and never had to put on makeup to look good. I'm still madly in love with her today.

She loved animals, but wasn't too keen on reptiles initially. Before long she was accompanying Stevo and me on trips up north. He reckoned Melinda drove a four-wheel-drive better than me. Later on, she handled snakes and crocs with guidance from us.

Stevo badly wanted to find Miss Right. His 'sexual deserts' remained a topic of discussion among us guys for years until he literally met his dream girl, a spunky American tourist who liked wildlife and camping. Their relationship would change his life.

*

Chris White remembers the drama in the air both in the lead-up to, and aftermath of, Steve and Mick's holiday. 'Steve wasn't as interested in the park while he was finishing his apprenticeship,' Whitey says. 'We all just wanted to go surfing. Then Steve, Mick and I made a pact we would sell everything we owned and go on this world trip.

'I was managing an insurance office at the time and decided I didn't want to leave Australia and return with nothing. So I piked. It didn't go down very well, especially considering we'd also fallen out a couple of years earlier when I criticised Steve and Mick's lifestyle. I guess I was Mr Conservative, got married and had kids early.'

Di Schwenke's enduring memory of Steve is dressed as a devil at his and Mick's going-away party on 26 May, before his devil-may-care attitude matured. Steve had borrowed Di's trusty pushbike at 3am to go to the shops at Dicky Beach. 'He came flying back into our place—again with flat tyres—saying the coppers were chasing him. Just imagine it. He was wearing full devil's makeup, red tights, red jocks and a tail.

'When we dropped them at the airport you could feel their excitement,' says Di. 'We'd gone through our travel albums with Steve. But he came back confused about where he wanted to go in life. A bit lost.'

Chris noticed it too. 'When Steve and my brother returned after six months, having only got as far as a resort hut in Thailand, the two of them went on a three-month expedition catching monitor lizards up in the Top End. I guess Steve was still finding himself. He returned full of renewed ambition to save animals and decided he wanted to be part of the park properly again. His parents were extremely happy.'

Chapter 8

'ere you are. Two black eyes for a wedding. Here, piggy. Missions from Bob. Leaping lizards. Gory wedgie. Spruced up for a Caloundra wedding.

A couple of days before Chris White was due to marry my sister at Caloundra on 6 June 1987, Stevo and I took Chilli and Rhino up to Nathan Gorge. We were weaving in the truck along a gravel road when a pig sprinted across. Rhino and I jumped out and gave chase.

A group of pigs took off. Some went right, towards an open field. I followed the ones that went left. Rhino and I bolted into the scrub, but the pigs disappeared. All of a sudden we were in unfamiliar, tight, whipstick country where everything looked the same.

I was lost. Every tree was the same size and shape. It was almost dark and the winter night was freezing.

Stevo tooted the horn. Didn't help much considering my dodgy hearing. I had no idea where it was. I said to Rhino, 'Get the truck, go to the truck,' but he ran in circles.

I yelled, 'Find Stevo,' and Rhino ran off. I followed him. He stopped and milled around me. I got a bit panicky and unloaded a couple of shots into the air.

Stevo called, 'Cooeee, cooee.'

'I don't know which direction you're coming from.' I kept yelling. About 20 minutes later Stevo appeared out of the icy blackness.

'Come on, you're right, no worries, Fris,' he laughed.

It wasn't until hours later that we noticed the blood all over my face.

When I'd jumped from the moving vehicle I'd hit the door and cut my head open. Already sporting a black eye from a recent boxing bout, I now had a lovely gash above the other one.

So for my sister's wedding I had a split face and two black eyes.

They're the sort of memories I cherish now. We had no money. We'd basically get the change out of the ashtray so we could afford to get a beer en route.

We'd spend days searching for special animals or doing chores around our makeshift camp, then at dusk we'd go shooting for croc food. Mates, guns and dogs: the chases were thrilling.

Sometimes we gave the people back home a glimpse of our secret world. Stevo stuck the head of a pig from Nathan Gorge on the front of his truck and drove around with it for a couple of weeks at Beerwah until the maggots reeked. Sometimes I'm not so sure people appreciated the glimpse.

Other times it was different. When Stevo and I travelled to Iron Range in late 1987, the fun and games all but disappeared. This was to become one of our most significant reptile trips—we found one of the rarest goannas in Australia.

This time the scientists were as excited as Stevo and me. Until then the Queensland Museum had only been able to study a few dead canopy goanna specimens (scientific name *varanus keithhornei,* previously *varanus teriae*) brought out of Cape York years earlier.

But the Stevo-Fris team managed to track down a healthy live specimen—using the Irwin smarts, my uncanny eyesight, a little luck and more human blood loss, of course.

*

The *teriae*, as we called it then, is the only Aussie monitor lizard with a prehensile tail. It lives in trees and uses its tail like a monkey to grasp branches when climbing, hanging or reaching for food. Other goannas don't have these multi-purpose tails.

It's carnivorous and prehistoric-looking, but shorter than a human arm—about 40 to 50 centimetres (15-19 inches) from head to tail with little gangly legs. This Queensland reptile is black with silver flecks across its scales. On a recent visit to Papua New Guinea I saw their close relative, the green tree monitor (*varanus prasinus*), which is an amazing shade of fluorescent green.

We were spending a couple of weeks in and around beautiful Iron Range National Park on missions from Bob, who had a government permit to collect a live specimen of a canopy goanna. To my bug-eyed, beaming mate, that was a Willy Wonka golden ticket. Bob told his son what animals he wanted, where to look, how to find them and what to do. Stevo sucked up all that information and processed it through me.

We scouted trees day and night for screeching Palm Cockatoos, nocturnal Green pythons and this damned elusive lizard. I was annoyed. We didn't even know if we'd recognise it because no one had seen one alive. For all I knew it was extinct.

Stevo the motivator said he loved taking me on these trips because while I might not have the ears, I had the eyes. I could always spot things, even travelling at 70 kilometres (45 miles) per hour. Suddenly I'd yell, 'Back up! I've seen it.'

He'd marvel, 'How'd you see that, Fris?'

This time, however, my powers of observation stalled and we called it quits. We started heading back to Weipa, about 250 kilometres (155 miles) west. We drove down a couple of gullies and as we climbed I said, 'Stop.'

'What?' Stevo hit the brakes on the dirt road, skidding to a halt.

'Look there, in the tree.'

We looked up. I still get goosebumps thinking about it, because I wasn't sure what I'd seen.

Stevo got out and scrambled up on the bullbar. We caught a glimpse of the rare lizard scooting around the back of a high branch, where it hid.

Boom! Stevo jumped.

If he had missed, we wouldn't have seen that animal for dust. But he caught it. It spun around, bit him on the wrist and locked on. That mouth was small but vicious.

'Wooohooo,' Stevo yodelled in delight, not pain. He knew he had a firm grip on the body and the tail had instinctively wrapped around his arm.

I was alarmed. 'It's got ya! It's got ya!'

'I've got it! I've got it!' he retaliated.

It kept biting him and the wound was ugly, but there was no way he was letting go. Blood streaked his clothes.

To me, it was just another goanna. I'd had previous conversations with Stevo, saying, 'Mate, the public would be happy if you just had bearded dragons, a crocodile and some snakes in the park. Half the visitors won't even know the difference.' Of course that didn't matter to him; he knew we would educate the public.

After an intense few minutes, Stevo got the *teriae* down and wrapped it snugly in a pillowslip. He told me the comfortable material would quieten the animal and reduce its stress.

Before leaving, we took photos of the fateful tree and pondered our luck. Had the truck stopped a metre forward he would have had to climb on the bonnet, giving the lizard more time to escape. Had it stopped a metre back he would have had to climb the tree, forcing the lizard up into the towering canopy. That Irwin knack with wildlife was the awesome part of these treks.

Upon our return we were shocked to hear that some experts wanted to kill the healthy *teriae* to cut it open and study its biology.

We wouldn't allow it. We hid our find until Bob and Stevo made a deal with the museum, which would study and photograph the creature's habits while it lived safely at the park.

For several months we collected its excreta for scientific examination. The museum people came to watch its feeding habits, especially the unusual way it used its front feet to wipe its face while eating. Stevo concluded that the habit stemmed from wiping away green ants that shared its home high above the rainforest.

In 1993, just after I had left the park, they caught another three specimens—two females and a male—and launched a breeding program. Although our little mate succumbed to cancer, by 1997 the park boasted the first successful captive reproduction of *varanus teriae* in the country. Current Australia Zoo curator Kelsey Engle published a paper about it.

*

Further north of Iron Range were other favourite lizard-seeking haunts: the Wenlock and Coen rivers to the west and Silver Plains cattle station to the south-east. I was stunned by the biodiversity of the dense green rainforests and wetlands of the Wenlock—and I've never swum in more spectacular waterfall locations in my life.

Stevo and I went there looking for Mertens water monitors because the park only had one, named Murdie. These goannas have flat tails for paddling. On this occasion we dipped out, but on a later pigging and fishing trip to Silver Plains with Melinda and Pete Usher, I was lucky enough to swim with a couple of Mertens.

Well, it was by accident. And only as I frantically yelled, 'Get outta the water!' All I could see were ominous heads gliding towards us in the river.

It was exciting a few years down the track when the Irwins managed to breed Mertens.

Part of the Wenlock catchment is now in the 135,000 hectare

(330,500 acre) Steve Irwin Wildlife Reserve. It's a parcel of land north-east of Weipa bought for $6 million by the Australian government in July 2007 so the Irwin family can manage it for conservation and preserve Steve's legacy.

The only problem is that a mining company intends to extract bauxite from part of it. As Terri Irwin and Cape Alumina take it through the courts, she's been focusing world attention on it with a global petition to prevent mining.

*

In 2009 it's almost impossible to believe how remote and politically incorrect things were a couple of decades ago in far north Queensland. Up around Coen the pubs were racially segregated.

There were white bars and black bars. You'd walk in the big front door and far off to the left was a little door with bars across it and that's where Aborigines bought their alcohol. Racism seemed to be accepted.

The one occasion I sensed a mood swing was on a holiday to the Weipa region with Melinda, Pete and Clive, who was best man at my wedding. I'd grown up with Clive, whose family lived at Diamond Head just around the corner from my place.

We arrived at a pub after a hectic day fishing and shooting. Three of us were busy tying tarps on the two HiLuxes. Clive, who had never been to that neck of the woods, said, 'Should I go in?'

'Yeah, sure. We'll be there in a minute,' I said.

Did I mention Clive's appearance? We called him Stick Man. A nice bloke and a hot surfer, but damn he was skinny. Hair so white that pool chlorine made it go green. A typical surfie, wearing a pink shirt and boardshorts.

Seconds later Clive rushed back out. He was even paler.

He had walked into the wrong bar. This slight white boy in pink had barged into a room full of muscle-bound Islanders and Aborigines and demanded a drink.

Apparently Clive turned tail when one of them said three words, 'You. Next door.'

It didn't get much better en route home.

The rains caught us while driving back and the track disappeared. Literally. All we could see was water and a gap in the melaleucas.

We couldn't turn the trucks around because we didn't know where the track ended so we just crawled through the trees. It was bloody hairy.

*

One of the most gruesome things I ever saw in the wild was in the late '80s, on a croc-trapping trip with Stevo to his beloved Camp Chilli near Ingham. He'd built a lean-to with a tin roof and a tarp, a basic but hardy structure which was still standing a few years ago despite the weather extremes. In the wet the camp became a slushy bog. Take a look at this photo of a previous visit, where flash flooding trapped us—and a croc in a box—until a tractor could tow us all out.

Camp Chilli: Bob and Stevo's legendary campsite near Cattle Creek became a swamp after it copped eight inches (20cm) of rain this night in the mid-'80s.

But on this occasion, in the dry, it was stinking hot on those parched saltpan flats. Only a couple of eucalypt and brushbox broke the burning landscape towards the mangroves.

We were sitting in the shade of the tarp, gazing up at wedge-tail eagles circling around.

I asked Stevo what they were doing.

'Oh, probably after wallabies in the paddock over there,' he said.

Doubtful, I got out my big scope on my rifle to get a better look and said, 'Yeah, there are wallabies over there.'

'One of those wedgies will take out a wallaby,' he said.

'What? It couldn't.'

I knew wedgies preyed on rabbits, roadkill and the occasional lamb, but surely not a marsupial of that size.

An hour later I watched a bird zoom down near the ground and make a hit.

'Stevo, he's got one.'

We ran over, startling the bird which flew into a nearby tree. Lying on the ground, still kicking, was a female sub-adult Agile wallaby. The sandy-coloured females grow to just under a metre and are identified by white stripes on their cheek and thigh.

The wedgie had taken the top of its head clean off. One side was scalped, leaving just the ear. I had never seen anything like it. As we left nature to its own horrible devices, the wedgie returned to its victim.

It made me think twice about laughing at Stevo the next time he got Mr-Wedgie-on-the-head back at the park.

*

Nineteen eighty-nine was a big year for me. At 24 years old, I married my sweetheart Melinda at Our Lady of the Rosary Church at Kings Beach. My groomsmen were my brother John-Paul, Stevo, Rod and Clive. Stevo brought his parents and his then girlfriend.

Watching my future wife walk down the aisle was very emotional, until she got close and I realised my sweating palms were actually dripping. The crowd watched me infamously wipe my hands down the sides of my hired suit before taking her hand when it was offered in front of the priest.

It was 25 February, a hot, sunny Sunshine Coast summer's day. Not so hot were the 25 to 30 knot winds. After the ceremony our wedding party and other close friends went to Shelley Beach for photos.

Disaster. The wind kept lifting the girls' dresses—though we boys couldn't see a problem with that—and blowing their hairstyles all over the shop. We couldn't wait to be done with it. An esky of refreshments was close at hand for stress relief.

Then we hit the Caloundra Civic Centre, just off the main street, for the reception. A posh and rather expensive wedding display in the foyer consisted of a groom in top hat and tails and a bride in a traditional gown. Let's just say that by the end of the evening several important bits were missing and revellers were on a trophy-hunting mission to avoid coughing up compensation.

Our night was true to form with family and friends celebrating our best day yet. My groomsmen couldn't wait to unwind after the formalities. We weren't accustomed to suits, nor to standing in front of everyone to make speeches.

Tony and Melinda Frisby's wedding reception at Caloundra Civic Centre, 25 February 1989. (L-R) Melinda, Beryl (Stevo's girlfriend at the time), Stevo, Bob and Lyn Irwin.

It was the first time I had seen Bob Irwin in dress pants and a collared good shirt. Stevo said it was the first time in years that Bob and Lyn had attended a social event outside the park. Check out the photo of Bob, Lyn and Stevo with Beryl, who he met while she was working at a cafe off the highway at Ingham. They spruced up, didn't they?

No prizes for guessing our honeymoon destination. Where else but Cape York? Melinda and I spent a magic three months exploring the stunning region. There was no escaping Stevo, who had drawn us a map with a list of instructions on animals to keep an eye out for. It was like a treasure hunt, although as newlyweds we were a bit distracted.

A couple of months later my new bride and I decided we wanted to be surrounded by nature and wildlife in the tropical north every day. We didn't have much money. As Melinda recalls too clearly, everything we owned was in the back of my HiLux Extra Cab truck.

But we remembered the amazing swimming and snorkelling around Dunk Island and Mission Beach, south of Cairns, discovered a few years earlier when I worked on Dunk for eight months. So we moved to Cairns, Queensland's most northern large city.

Cairns is on the east coast, the last stop on the Bruce Highway after a 22-hour, 1700-kilometre (1055-mile) drive from the Brisbane capital. Hyped as the gateway to both the rainforests of Cape York Peninsula and the waters of the Great Barrier Reef, the region has spent decades balancing the interests of tourism, the environment, agriculture and development. One of those commercial interests was Hartley's Creek Crocodile Farm and by the second half of 1989 I was in the thick of the action as its curator/showperson.

Caloundra High, year 12, Steve is in the back row, left.

Eighties style: Stevo and Gary's combined 21st at the 'party house', complete with out-of-control food fight, Caloundra, February 1983.

Another weekend, another party: young Stevo (R) with a couple of friends.

Hamming it up: at another gathering in the mid-80s.

Game on: the Kings Beach crew after they battled Moffat Beach in footy. Stevo is on the far right with the bandage. He always used his head!

Sun, sand & surf: Stevo enjoying Kings Beach, Caloundra.

Stevo surfs Kings Beach.

What's in the box? Transferring one of the first big crocs into the Queensland Reptile and Fauna Park, early '80s. The croc had been caught way up north in Bamaga. Middle photo shows (L-R, holding crate lid): Stevo, Bob Irwin, Steve G and Tony Frisby.

Strike a pose: Stevo under the tent annexe at Fraser Island, and under the ute canopy at Double Island Point on the mainland, both early '80s.

Great shot, Stevo: a Central Netted Dragon.

Gotcha: Stevo catches a Spencer's monitor on one of our trips to western Queensland, mid '80s.

Awash in the Wenlock: Stevo makes the most of some Wenlock River waterfalls in Queensland's far north, 1988.

600kg of Agro: the territorial, lawnmower-hating croc that Stevo and Chili dog caught at Cattle Creek in the late '80s pictured in his new home, the Crocodile Environmental Park at Beerwah in 1991.

How high? Stevo asks me to climb on the truck to show the extraordinary height of this termite mound, Cape York, 1989.

Setting the net: Stevo and I croc-trapping, Cattle Creek, late '80s.

Silent Bob: Tony examines a couple of fresh yellow belly fish while camped in central western Queensland with Bob Irwin.

Tropical paradise: Stevo and I park the 4WD at a favourite Cape York location, Chili Beach on the edge of the crystal clear Coral Sea.

Science comes alive: Stevo admires a rare live specimen of a canopy goanna, or *varanus teriae*, found in Cape York, late 1987.

Tony with Albert the Alligator, Queensland Reptile and Fauna Park, early '90s. At this time I was a curator helping launch a gator breeding program.

Iguanas on patrol: Tony gets up close and personal with iguanas at the Queensland Reptile and Fauna Park, early '90s.

Gonna need a bigger boat: Tony uses all his croc skills to capture this 15-footer (4.5-metres) north of Cooktown in 1997. The croc had to be removed by the Queensland Parks and Wildlife Service after it took up residence in a popular kids' swimming hole near Hope Vale.

Watch out for the trunk: Stevo introduces the elephants to Tony and his young son Nathan, along with Tony's sister Mandy White (R), at Australia Zoo, 2004.

Chapter 9

Putting the 'rock' in croc. Scars and death rolls. 'Excellento, we've got Bogie'. In the name of science. Stevo's dive of faith. Jibba gets filthy.

Hartley's Creek Crocodile Farm, where I worked from 1989 to September 1990, was north of Cairns at a small beach town called Wangetti. Its location was ideal to snare visitors travelling the 65 kilometres (40 miles) between Cairns and Port Douglas on the Captain Cook Highway, one of Australia's most picturesque ocean roads. (Wangetti even achieved international TV fame in 2003 as a location in *The Amazing Race*.)

Now a major attraction called Hartley's Crocodile Adventures, even back then it had saltie and snake shows, cassowary feeding, and diverse wetland wildlife on display. We caught rogue crocs and bred them in captivity. But I quickly noted differences with the Beerwah sanctuary.

Sitting uncomfortably with my wildlife protection philosophies picked up from the Irwins was the simple fact that this was a working farm. Crocs, like domestic cattle elsewhere, were killed to produce skins and raw meat for export—and local restaurant tables. Heavy discussions took place about methods of croc farming. I felt torn as I helped raise beautiful animals which were destined to be culled for meat production or leathering.

I've had to argue the pros and cons of this industry many times since. At backyard barbies, someone will ask me, 'So what's a croc steak taste like?' I've never eaten it and I don't intend to. Like the ol' vegetarian versus carnivore debate, people on either side will never agree.

Bob Irwin always hated crocodile farming because of the greed and barbarism of mavericks in the industry. His son made his own views clear to a national audience in 2003 on the ABC's *Australian Story*.

Stevo attacked his critics, calling them 'wildlife perpetrators' who hid behind terms like 'sustainable use'. He said, 'People [who] think that by eating crocodiles and whales that we'll actually save the world...that is bullshit and that is bad and it is something that must stop.'

In that same year, a federal senate inquiry into the commercial use of native wildlife noted that the Australian croc farming industry, started in 1972 by the federal government as a job creation project at an Aboriginal community in north Queensland, had been worth A$1.5 million in 1990.

The Irwins were never driven by money. 'You can't put a price on the head of any animal,' was a philosophy Bob, Stevo and Lyn had taught and shown me. They were adamant, sincere and direct about it.

If a turtle was sick, the same effort went into saving it whether that species was a dime-a-dozen or endangered. When we got permits from the government to search for Green pythons in Iron Range National Park in the '80s, Bob and Stevo were disgusted to learn that the black market priced the snakes at up to $10,000 each. We all knew that animals illegally traded usually suffered and often died.

And when it came to crocs, nothing was too much trouble if it meant sparing the animal discomfort. If that meant a 2800-kilometre (1740-mile), non-stop, round trip from Beerwah to Ingham to pick up a newly-trapped saltie, so be it.

*

Hartley's Creek was progressive in many ways. It was one of the first attractions in Australia to hold fair dinkum crocodile attack shows, including death rolls, as tourist entertainment. Owner Harry Freeman, his son Peter, the manager, and their staff taught me how to be a showperson rather than just an animal keeper. My recipe mixed one part humour and one part excitement with two parts education.

I already had Stevo to thank for my conservation values and physical experiences of working with crocs, so I concentrated on honing these skills while adding rock 'n' roll thrills for the public.

I practised with a young employee named Drew. Gung-ho and daring, we competed to see who could get closest to the larger crocodiles without losing part of our anatomy. When feeding an 11-foot (3.4-metre) male named Yard, we took turns at holding the chook as high as possible. If Yard clipped us or landed on our feet on his way down after the jump, it meant top marks.

When the public arrived, we went into action with Scarsides, a 13-footer (4 metres) who bore white scars on his back where a tin shed had blown on him in a tropical cyclone. As people walked in the front gate towards a stand running parallel to a muddy pond, I would ask, 'Anyone see a crocodile?' and stamp my foot. (That's how I later taught Stevo to do it with Murray the croc.)

Scarsides would come flying out of the pond. Everyone gasped. I dangled a piece of cowhide tied to a rope, usually flipping it in time to avoid a direct hit. Slap! The saltie's jaws snapped shut, empty. Everyone sighed in relief.

The exhibition continued. Scarsides submerged. Drew and I jumped across to a little island in the enclosure. The croc stalked us through the long grass. We jumped back. One of us threw the cow hide to Scarsides and pulled on the rope while the other kept watch, ready to step in if he launched too fast.

The climax. The death roll. People watched in awe as Scarsides did 360s in the shallows as we explained how this would drown a buffalo or cow so the croc could dismember it for feasting.

Tug-of-war: Tony and Scarsides at the Hartley's Creek Crocodile Farm

Then there was Norton. His enclosure was the most exciting for Hartley's staff because 'he had the taste'. Norton was notorious for ripping off a keeper's arm, long before I worked there. We dared each other to remove any uneaten food from his pond. That meant wading out with a gaff hook and your heart in your mouth. I mean, we didn't even wear shoes. This was way before modern regulations.

I remember getting in trouble from Harry when he found out about another display. Granted, it was a bit off. But people found it hilarious.

In front of a sizeable crowd, I enticed Scarsides close to the fence with a freshly slaughtered chicken. These were laying hens that had finished their working lives at a poultry farm.

Whack! Scarsides chomped down on the chook. The pressure forced a last egg to shoot out of its bum. Smack! The egg exploded on the fence, splattering anyone nearby. The stink was dreadful. Sometimes I thought Scarsides was in on it, especially when he did a big tail splash, spraying dirty water over the crowd.

The farm was fun, but I knew they were gearing up for the first mass cull since I'd been there. It takes five years to get a crocodile from birth to handbag. They had built up the stock and the equipment was ready. I was struggling to direct my public talks towards crocodile physiology, habits and myth-busting rather than the impending 'harvest' and what might be on the menu at the restaurant. I still couldn't come to grips with that side of it. I learnt a lot there, but ultimately it wasn't for me. The experience shaped my future direction.

*

During my annual leave it wasn't hard to decide what to do or where to go. Croc catching with Stevo, of course. I couldn't get enough. We even made the local paper with one of our trips to the Burdekin River region, south of Ingham and our favourite haunt of Cattle Creek.

We arrived in the early afternoon at a junction of the Burdekin and Bowen rivers. Stevo had received reports of a dangerous crocodile in an area backing on to a Brahman cattle stud. He asked if I wanted to take a look. With my newfound cockiness, I said, 'Yeah, no worries.'

We had to get out and half-push, half-pull our flatbottom punt across the almost-dry, dirty brown Burdekin. You couldn't see anything below the surface.

Suddenly I shouted, 'Look look look!'

We had reached the mouth of the Bowen. By the time Stevo followed my pointing finger, a huge croc had slid off the bank into the water.

'Mate! How big do you think it was?' he said.

'Between 12 and 13 foot (3.5-4 metres), if not bigger,' I said.

'Hell animal.'

We checked out its slide, parked the boat on the sandbar, walked up behind some trees and sat there until sunset. There was a flying fox colony on the left bank heading into the junction and at twilight they took off en masse.

It was one giant black cloud of stench, that's for sure. Dozens of these bats were swooping down and clipping the water, scooping up mouthfuls to drink.

Whoosh! The water exploded, like someone let off a bomb. This croc launched from underneath, taking a potshot at a flying fox before crashing back down.

I don't know if he succeeded. It was too dark and fast. We didn't see him resurface to swallow it. But he may have eaten it behind overhanging trees, hidden from our view. Forget that idea of crocs storing their food under riverbanks for days before chowing down. That's a fallacy—they like their tucker fresh. Crocs are opportunistic and will eat carrion but, like most animals, they prefer fresh food.

The next day we returned and set up the bag trap under the flying fox colony. After our previous misadventure in a bat camp, we felt vindicated in baiting the trap with their fresh corpses. Under the colony we also found a beautiful, swollen, carpet snake. Stevo admiringly said it had chosen a perfect location for feeding on sick or young flying foxes that dropped from the branches.

I appreciated the fact that those observation skills and hunter's knowledge were passed down from Bob to Stevo to me. We knew, for example, there was no use baiting this trap with pork because the croc was eating bats. The challenge was everything. To me, it felt like the competitive rush of playing footy against a guy who has the edge on you.

When you match yourself against a master in its environment, you've gotta know what it eats, shits, does, sleeps, thinks. You must respect the status, the pecking order in the wild. When you target an animal, it's your knowledge and physical ability against them and the elements.

The bag trap worked. We named the big croc Bogie, got him secured and settled, then rushed to the nearby farming community of Dalbeg. We knew we'd need assistance to get this fella on the train to Beerwah. Neither of us pondered how bizarre such requests must have seemed to friendly locals. Funny thing is, we rarely got knockbacks.

'Steve and Tony rushed into our shop, yelled "we've got a croc and need help to bring it back" and there was a huge expedition mounted,' recalls fruit and vegetable grower Lorelle McShane. Lorelle and her husband Sean still run the Dalbeg Inn and McShane's Produce on the Burdekin River, about 150 kilometres (93 miles) south of Townsville and inland from Bowen. The McShane family had arrived from Northern Ireland in the 1950s, growing tobacco and sugarcane, and they were known for their lively pub and tours. Lorelle, Sean and the kids were often in the thick of things during these trips by me and Stevo before he hit the big time.

'About 10 farmers and as many Eskies were loaded up on utes for the adventure,' recalls Lorelle. 'Keeping Bogie cool and wet, they brought him back and tied him up under the trees out the front. While we waited for Parks and Wildlife to come and record him, the word got out. "There's a croc at the shop!" Many people turned up for a look. Eventually Steve and Tony crated Bogie and put him on the rail.'

Lorelle remembers our captures of almost a dozen crocodiles over a season. 'There was Bogie, Bluey, Molly, Connie, Sharon and about six smaller ones,' she lists. 'Two were named after my children, Molly and Connar. Sharon was the daughter of our friend Des. The day Steve and Tony caught Connie, I cooked them bacon and eggs as we sat chatting and waiting for Parks and Wildlife. My young daughters climbed all over Steve and teased Tony, playing with his hair.

'Steve always had a lot of time for the kids and I know he would have been a great dad. We still find it hard to believe he is no longer on this earth. He was so focused and involved in his work, I never believed he would die from what he loved.'

Lorelle says our visits and the Irwin wildlife philosophy certainly left an impression.

'Thanks to Steve and Tony, we had many different animals at our house over the years. Molly loved everything—including snakes—and dreamed of working at the Irwin zoo. Steve taught me not to be afraid of snakes and how to deal with them. It took me a long time but now I just push them out of the house without a problem.'

Of course there was a lot of fun and camaraderie among all that serious reptile-handling in the Burdekin.

'Steve and Tony were eccentric but normal blokes who liked a drink and a good time even though they were croc hunters and wildlife lovers,' Lorelle says. 'They camped down the river and I guess we were the central social location.

'Steve's favourite saying was "excellento". He would literally bounce into the shop early in the morning and declare, "Hello Lorelle, have you got any bacon? Excellento!" Tony was quieter, probably overshadowed by Steve's exuberance.'

Evenings at the Dalbeg Inn ranged from 'strip pool' to the odd blue—well, a regular named Bluey anyway. Sean McShane recalls, 'One night Tony and Steve joined Bluey, Bill and Mad Jeff for a beer. They challenged a couple of female staff to pool. The rules were clear. Anyone who didn't pot a ball during the entire game had to remove their top. So the ladies did.'

In walked Lorelle. 'The boys were still in a state of shock when I came home from a P&C meeting,' she smiles.

'I remember another long-ish night when Steve was drinking his Powers Bitter and we were watching a girl get more and more upset with Bluey's comments. Just when we thought she was going to punch him out, Steve stepped in and talked her down. It was hilarious listening to him.'

The McShanes also saw how much Steve idolised his dad. 'He was so excited when Bob turned up one day, he nearly fell off his seat. Steve quickly hid his beer and put out his cigarette. He couldn't wait to introduce his dad to us.'

*

The intensity and repetition of these croc captures further stirred Stevo's natural scientific bent. I remember him pointing out that Bogie had four scutes (bony plates) on the back of his neck. Every other saltie we'd caught had six. It was the kind of observation that usually started Stevo on a line of questioning or fact-finding that resulted in expanded knowledge about our native crocs. He desperately wanted to replace people's hatred of them with greater understanding.

This didn't wash with some critics and scientists at the time, though. They looked down their noses at his knowledge, which was unashamedly based on simple field work and observation.

The joke was on them years later, as 'that Crikey bastard' received local, national and international recognition for this behind-the-scenes persistence. The importance and accuracy of his work resulted in not just scientific collaborations and papers, but academic awards.

He ended up working closely with top professors, scientists and other experts from across the world. The University of Queensland posthumously named him an Adjunct Professor in Integrative Biology. He had conducted croc research expeditions with UQ's Professor Craig Franklin, who later paid tribute to Stevo's 'great mind—creative and complex and driven by curiosity' (*Sunshine Coast Daily,* Memories of Steve tribute, 2007).

In 2000 he was appointed an Honorary Senior Fellow of the University of the Sunshine Coast. (So was Terri in 2007, for her contribution to wildlife conservation.) The university's Vice Chancellor Paul Thomas described Stevo's delight at receiving the honour in his hometown, how he whooped and punched the air on stage at the ceremony. 'The university was very early on interested in Steve's views and actions on conservation, animal rehabilitation, his wildlife knowledge and communication skills,' Professor Thomas said. 'There was never any serious doubt about the value of his work.'

In 2004 Stevo was named Queensland's finalist for Australian of the Year. Former premier Peter Beattie presented him with the award at a gala event. Stevo wore his khakis.

Yet even in death, Stevo can't escape the doubters. As I write this chapter in the summer of 2008-09, public argument is raging about the croc satellite tracking study he'd started with university and state government researchers in north Queensland. Despite its valuable research on the movements of estuarine crocodiles, the whole study is in question after the discovery of a relocated croc near heavily populated Magnetic Island, off Townsville.

Understandably, some people reacted with fear. Some wanted to ban the study.

However, to me, it helps prove another Stevo theory—that older, territorial crocs always try to make their way home in the wild. That's why we spent all those years working with rangers to shift the big 'uns to safe, fenced, private sanctuaries such as the humble Beerwah park. To keep the public and the crocs safe.

*

About this time in late 1990, our Caloundra mate Jeff 'Jibba' Allchin got his first taste of croc-trapping up north. He seemed to have fun but never repeated it. Wonder why? As the 48-year-old Currimundi married father of three now recalls:

'It was a kind of boys' reunion. Steve had returned to his regular camp at the mouth of Cattle Creek on another East Coast Crocodile Management Program mission. Mick and I drove up from Beerwah to join him for a week. It had been a while since I'd caught up with Tony, who was living in Cairns, so he and his father John drove down to camp for that first weekend.

'Before Mick and I left we visited Lyn Irwin at the zoo and asked if she'd like us to take anything up to Steve. "Just make sure he looks after that leg," she repeated sternly. It was about six weeks after Steve's infamous run-in with the she-croc he named Joan Collins. We knew how nasty the bite had been—Steve had delighted in showing us the video he taped by himself.

'"Boys, you gotta see this, it's a really good one," he had boasted as he pressed play in the living room. We watched Steve crawl into a box in remote bushland, promptly followed by a big saltwater croc that snapped down on his calf. We rolled up laughing as the tape recorded his swearing, though he didn't miss a beat and completed the capture.

'"You're an idiot," we roared. "You've gotta put that on *Funniest*

Home Videos, you'll make a fortune." As history showed, it screened on TV and made him a squillion all right—but as part of his own documentary series.

'When I hung out with Steve that week at Camp Chilli, I certainly noticed the two weeping holes on his lower leg. They were oozing and often submerged in dirty mud for hours. But how the hell do you tell Steve Irwin to look after himself?

'When I got to camp, Tony and Steve were pleased because they'd just caught a big croc and put it on the train back to Beerwah. Mick and I went out in the boat to check on a trap Steve had set at the end of Cattle Creek. A rotting pig's head dangled from a tree in the warm spring sun. It was the leading bait, set above a vertical riverbank that was about 1.5 metres (5 feet) high at low tide. Mick pointed out why Steve had chosen that location. Gouged into the wall of mud were claw and slide marks. I was shocked by the claw size—much bigger than my hand.

'Once we reported the activity to Steve, he turned into Action Man. I took photos as he cleared a sizeable spot on the bank, slashing into the bush, so he could hitch up the 16-tonne scallop-net bag trap. He said: "C'mon, we'll zip down the creek and get the sandbag I've prepared." We used sandbags as counterweights to pull the drawstrings of the trap tightly closed.

'By the time we returned the tide was in and lapping over the top of the riverbank. Steve peered at the surface. "He's watching us, you know. He's heard all the commotion and he's checking his territory." I couldn't see squat in the murky water.

'Our boat slid into the bank, level with the trap. Growing in confidence, I volunteered to take the sandbag into the mangroves. Mick also came ashore. Then Steve jumped over to tie the sandbag and haul it up to a high branch. The three of us returned to the water's edge. Guess where the boat was?

'"I'm not getting it," Mick yelled. "Me neither," I said.

'Someone had forgotten to tie up the tinnie. It had floated out to the middle. The creek was only 20 metres (65 feet) wide but you'd have to be an idiot to risk a swim. That meant we were stranded in a croc's bloodied lair. My eyes popped as Steve ripped off his shirt, dived into the water, swam out and pulled himself on board. I've never seen a guy stroke so fast and flip himself straight over the side of a boat.

'Unfortunately we were destined for disappointment and missed catching that croc. I understand it was the same one that Steve and Terri later found shot dead when they were on their Queensland honeymoon.'

*

Jibba describes life at Camp Chilli as an education. 'We were surrounded by sugarcane, cattle and scrub on the northern bank of Cattle Creek. The nearest civilisation was a little town on the Bruce Highway called Rollingstone. The five of us had a ball but every bit of fun had an element of fear. Sometimes a rather large element. Fishing at night, for example, meant navigating between the reflection of crocodile eyes.

'Tony and John provided us with an amazing meal one night. They'd caught coral trout and mud crabs while skin diving and cut the backstrap from a baby pig they'd shot. So we all dined on pork and gourmet seafood. I decided I'd join the boys snorkelling one morning.

'We took the boat out to snorkel near fringing coral reefs. Visibility was difficult, however, because the spring tides were slowly flushing dirt from the river mouth. Tony and Steve had told me about the crayfish they caught when the water was clear. Suddenly Steve goes, "Yeah, there was a big tiger shark here the other day." He spoke like a tour guide making a simple observation. I was straight back in the boat. Even though I'd been spear fishing with Steve in shark-infested waters at Double Island Point before, I wasn't going to tempt fate with a tiger, second only to the white pointer on the scary scale.

'Another morning we were charging around in my ute looking for pigs. Mick was beside me and Steve was in the back with his dog. Steve yells, "Stop stop stop Jibba!"

'Before I finished the skid, he and the dog were gone. When I caught up, Steve had hold of an angry sand goanna trying to run up a tree. It was so big even Steve's hands couldn't fit around the base of its tail. "Wait boys, I'll get it," he yelled as it burrowed into a hole in the hollow trunk.

'"You're not putting that thing in my ute," I declared half-heartedly. I was grateful to have Steve in the ute when my alternator died one night, though. Every time I turned on the headlights, the motor weakened and backfired. Pockets of campers thought we were shooting at them. "I know this road," said Steve. So he got behind the wheel, I stood in the back wielding a torch and we drove 15 kilometres (9 miles) from the Bruce Highway to camp with no headlights and no moonlight to guide us.

'Practical jokes were always high on the agenda. Steve made Mick and me filthy over one little number. And I mean filthy, literally. Because it was technically still the dry season, Steve insisted that we didn't waste water while camping that week. "There's no water to spare," he kept telling us. I'd brought two 20-litre (5-gallon) drums of water but he said we couldn't waste it on showers. Each day we'd sweat in the heat, handling pig corpses and thigh-deep in stinking mangrove mud, then try to wash off the worst of it in saltwater while watching for crocs.

'I couldn't work out how Steve stayed so much cleaner than me. Then it clicked. He had set traps near Townsville and whenever he drove there to check them, he'd stop at a roadhouse and have a lovely shower on the way back! By my fifth day Steve relented and suggested I bathe in a dam on this farmer's property. A cattle property. As I waded in I realised it was full of cow poo and my legs were covered in brown slime.

'Enough was enough. On the Thursday night I grabbed my water drum and filled the makeshift shower bag. Rain from heaven. Mick and I took Steve home with us, so at least Lyn got him back in one piece.'

Chapter 10

Snakes on a HiLux. The bullet that missed. Money for something. Did we cross the line, Bob? 'This is a really dangerous area'. Fangs, sister.

As Jibba found at Cattle Creek, simple things often turned into surreal dramas when you went bush with Stevo. On a different occasion in the Burdekin, Stevo and I were driving around trying to find bait. We arranged to meet a farmer not far from our camp to help us find a local flying fox colony.

We were standing there chatting when a chocolate taipan slithered from a gully to our left on to the ridge where we were parked. Stevo snatched it up. 'Wow look at this, a beautiful snake, healthy isn't it?'

'Yeah,' I said reluctantly. Real nice. 'C'mon Stevo, we better get moving.'

He let it go. It went straight under our vehicle, in behind the rear wheel and wrapped angrily around it. Taipans are the second most venomous snakes in Australia and this one was a couple of metres (almost 7 feet). A big sucker.

'What're you gonna do now?' I admonished. 'I told ya to leave the bloody thing alone.'

It was 35 degrees (95 Fahrenheit) in the shade. We were on hot, black sand on the edge of the Burdekin River with jabbing mosquitoes everywhere. Anyone else would have walked away and sought shelter until the snake decided to pack up its ol' kit bag. Or they would have driven away, ignoring the snake and hoping it fell off. Not Stevo.

'Well, let's take the tyre off,' he said.

He opened up the HiLux seat and got the jack. Mind you, this snake was ropable and half-hidden behind the brake well. Stevo was horizontal under the car, swearing and sweating and trying to set up the jack. Advantage: Snake.

It didn't strike but definitely contemplated it. An hour and a half later, Stevo had jacked it up, removed the wheel and shifted the snake without being fanged. Game: Stevo. Wild stuff.

*

It reminded me of another dodgy snake encounter on a trip to Cattle Creek in the late '80s. Stevo and I went diving in the Pacific. We knew there were heaps of resident crocodiles, yet there we were in scuba gear about 200 metres (650 feet) south of the river mouth and 100 metres (330 feet) offshore.

I was intent on finding crayfish but visibility was less than a metre as water rushed out of the mouth. Of all the threats I anticipated, Stevo plucked another from the ocean—literally.

I surfaced to see him playing fearlessly with a light tan and cream-coloured sea snake.

I admired snakes, especially the high quality ones at our park such as non-venomous, reticulated and Burmese pythons, but I did not enjoy handling them like Stevo or Wes did. I'd never willingly touch such a highly toxic creature in its own environment.

'The bloody thing's gonna bite you,' I said.

'No no, it'll be right,' Stevo said, running its thin body through his fingers.

'Then I'm outta here.'

Sea snakes have to breathe air but they are super agile in the water with front fangs that kill fish easily and rapidly. I swam to the boat. He didn't get bitten. Irwin Intuition struck again.

*

Meanwhile, my old mate the Burdekin River farmer decided to accompany us to our destination, the flying fox site. The three of us got in our front seat. It was so squishy I had to put my arm around the seat while this farmer sat his shotgun beside me. I looked at it and said, 'The gun's not loaded mate, is it?'

'Nah, nah, mate,' he said.

'No worries.'

As Stevo reversed back I noticed the farmer's four-wheel-drive had a bullet hole in the driver's door.

'What happened there?' I asked.

'Oh, rifle went off in the car,' he said.

So we arrived at the site and this farmer went to cock his shotgun. Nonchalantly, he muttered, 'Oh there's already one in it.'

Shocked, I looked at Stevo. Sometimes we were more scared of the locals than the damn animals. Make no mistake, the people we met on these trips were genuine, hospitable and generous. Just don't lose the bullets, okay?

*

Visitors from around the world now sit in Australia Zoo's 5000-seat Crocoseum to watch spectacular croc and alligator behaviour in carefully-orchestrated stadium shows. But the stadium almost never happened.

Eighteen years ago, park owner and Irwin patriarch, Bob wasn't keen on the idea of potentially dangerous feeding tricks for the public.

Stevo and I knew his dad's focus was on quietly improving reptile welfare and breeding programs. So it took a little convincing...and boy did we risk incurring the boss's wrath.

In December 1990, my friendship with Stevo brought Melinda and me back to the Sunshine Coast as I took the job of curator at the Irwins' Queensland Reptile and Fauna Park. The job offer felt wonderful because it recognised and rewarded what I'd done voluntarily for the park.

I didn't care that the pay was about $30 a week lower than Hartley's Creek. I had never been a paid-up employee at Beerwah before and $200 a week in the hand was nothing to sniff at. (Bob had said many times previously that he wished he could afford to hire me full-time.) For me, it was coming home to a zoo that did everything for the right reasons. Volunteering is a tradition there to this day.

Fangs for the help: Stevo and Tony practise a demonstration with the American alligators known as the Fang sisters in the early days of the zoo.

Melinda had enjoyed her job on the Port Douglas tourist boat Quicksilver Connections. But she'd chatted to so many visitors about our bush adventures with Steve Irwin that she also couldn't wait to return to Beerwah. (Incidentally she was fairly selective about mentioning the

Irwin name to locals, who branded him a wild card at that point.)

The curator position had been vacated by Wes, a young bloke I'd previously known as the work experience kid obsessed with snakes. About eight years younger than Stevo, Wes was a fixture at the park from the mid-1980s on.

He would get his parents to drop him off at weekends. Impressed, Stevo would tell me how Wes was 'a sponge, sucking up all the information'.

After Stevo took him under his wing like a little brother, Wes became a reptile expert and was appointed curator at 19 years old. He quit to travel overseas and expand his skills.

Wes later returned with a wealth of experience and worked his way up to become the current director of Australia Zoo and its 550 staff. He's now one of the best reptile keepers in the world—due in no small part to his own croc-catching jaunts with Stevo.

The only other non-family member working at the park full-time was Steve G as the second curator. An Irwin family friend who had been there for about 10 years, he was an extremely meticulous guy. Visitors to the park in the 1970s and 1980s would not have trodden on a single piece of kangaroo poo despite up to 18 roos roaming the grounds.

We respected Steve G's perfectionism but it strained relations a bit. Sometimes he demanded the park be raked twice a day to remove debris and droppings. At least once a day, if the wind blew 5 knots or better, we raked for leaves. Every morning the paths would get blown and washed off with hoses.

It was neat as a pin but at times our rituals were so overdone the concrete paths became exposed as the grass and earth fell away.

*

Barely weeks into my job, I was in Stevo's ear about ways to make more money to keep the park afloat. I saw it as a necessity, not a luxury, because we were only getting a handful of people through a day. Twenty visitors on a Saturday made news. Bob didn't care if it was quiet—he didn't much like people walking on his grass. He wasn't interested in attracting the coaches full of international tourists that regularly travelled to the Big Pineapple. They might mess things up.

However that meant, for example, we couldn't pay for pathology results to study the reasons for any animal sicknesses. It meant some of our equipment was cobbled together rather than state-of-the-art. It meant we had to wheel and deal just to get enough food for our expanding crocodile population.

We bred rats and mice as staples, but the fast-growing reptiles relocated from the bush needed more meat. Father and son had arranged to get dead chooks from local poultry farmers. Stevo and I would pick up half a dozen fertiliser bags full of them, tip them on the grass, bury any that were too far gone and sort the rest into correct sizes to feed individual crocs and snakes.

The Irwins had bred their first croc in the early 1980s. By 1987 we had finished constructing a fabulous series of ponds, pathways, bridges and enclosures christened the Crocodile Environmental Park. By the turn of 1990-91 more improvements were underway for the 150 hand-raised and relocated wild crocodiles and alligators.

I recall how deeply satisfied Stevo was to see his 'girls and boys' in their designer home. It was one of the few times I saw him in a chilled-out, reflective mood. When everyone else had left the park he would sit in front of the static display, have a couple of beers and just watch what the crocs did. He wouldn't say a word. Sui the dog would sit with him.

I couldn't understand why the park only rarely did feeding demonstrations for the public. The success of Hartley's Creek shows had taught me their value as both a public awareness tool and a crowd generator. Seriously, who doesn't like seeing a crazy man wield a chunk of raw meat to entice an apex predator? Especially one that can deliver a snapping bite many times stronger than a great white shark.

Stevo was ultra keen, but we hit a stumbling block with Bob. Until one day, Mr Irwin Senior went on holidays.

And we started doing demos for the public.

When Bob returned, we were all sitting around our smoko table. Stevo walked over carrying a calico bag full of money and plonked it on the table.

Bob carefully rolled a smoke. He looked at the bag and said, 'What's in there?'

Understandable, really. You never knew what the hell would be produced from inside a calico bag.

'That's what we've made while you've been away,' Stevo said.

'How'd you do that?'

'Watch, Tony's going to do a feed this afternoon!'

'Geez. Thanks Stevo, thanks,' I said.

Bob only watched halfway through my demo that afternoon and walked away. I was bloody terrified. Let there be no doubt, Bob's always been in charge of that zoo and what he said, went. He didn't need to say much. I never heard him say, to me or to Stevo, 'Don't ever do that.' It was his aura again. You knew it was wrong or if you were confused, he would sit you down and talk it out.

To our enormous relief, Bob decided to overlook our cheekiness and agreed to a crocodile and alligator feeding show program.

*

The Crocodile Environmental Park was designed to replicate natural habitat so the crocs felt comfortable and behaved normally to better educate the public. There were salties, freshies, juveniles and gators. A focal point was Agro, the 4.5-metre (15-foot) dominant male that Stevo and Chilli had brought back from Cattle Creek in the late '80s.

Agro patrolled his new territory including the nests of several lady friends—Mary, Cookie and Joan Collins. When we did presentations in Murray the saltie's adjoining enclosure, Agro watched silently.

'See those bubbles?' I'd say, pointing to Agro's pond. 'That's a real big croc.' People lined the fences waiting to see Agro cruise past.

When we crossed the boardwalk, chaining it to stop visitors following, Agro either blew more bubbles and waited for us to deliver his food or launched an attack. If we ran across, attack was a dead cert. And if Agro grabbed the supporting telegraph pole, he shook the whole deck.

The danger was that one of his girls would swim into the same area. Stevo, Steve G and I took turns at being each other's spotter. 'Stop! Cookie's comin', get outta there.' There's no chivalry in croc-land. If a female fought Agro for food, he'd kill her in a single crunch.

The whole thing took off. Fast and furious. And we charged people extra to enter the croc zone. Whenever I had a crowd at animal feeding time in the main part of the zoo I delivered my spiel:

'Look, if you want to see more, over this way we have 150 crocodiles and you can see them operating in a natural environment. We've got a static display showing you where and how we've caught these crocodiles.

'We've got a trap set up and we'll show you that. We'll tell you about crocodile behaviour. Anyone who's interested, tickets at the gate. We'll be leaving in 10 minutes.'

People ran. I kid you not.

Little did we know that in October 1991, one of those people rushing for an admission ticket would become Stevo's bride. He didn't need a nightclub after all!

The park went from hosting half a dozen people to a couple of hundred on weekends. Those numbers meant we always needed extra staff to keep people safe and off the fences. At the first enclosure my showmanship kicked in. 'See if you can see the crocodile in the murky water,' I encouraged the crowd. They'd be leaning over the fence, looking.

Then I stamped my foot, prompting 3-metre (10-foot) Murray to launch out of the water and lunge at that same fence. People flew backwards, hitting the far fence in fright, and if Mary was nesting nearby she then hurtled at them. It always got everyone laughing and babbling.

'Now I need you to stay off the fences,' I would say abruptly. 'Pay attention because this is a really dangerous area.' I knew I had their undivided attention, which was the perfect opportunity for education.

Stevo and/or I would continue the tour, explaining the importance of crocodilians in our ecosystem, and feeding certain ones depending on the time of year. When we reached the trap, our aim was to ensure everyone knew where the park animals had come from and the methods we used to catch them.

Stevo planted a forked tree in the sub-adult enclosure to display the working trap. We described the importance of a croc slide in planning a trap location, and the difference between a food slide and a sunning slide. What prey does this croc seek out? Where does he feel safe to leave the water and elevate his body temperature?

We explained why these sub-adults had been removed from built-up areas and how we caught them by jumping out of boats at night.

'You two really do that in the wild?' people marvelled.

We got more and more interstate and overseas visitors. Always happy to bite the hands that fed us, Stevo and I couldn't resist taking the piss out of Americans about their alligators.

'Americans think these guys are tough but they're little pussycats,' we smiled, patting the nearest gator on the head in their enclosure. Stevo often carted around a placid juvenile named Albert we got from Gosford Reptile Park. Albert turned out to be Alberta.

The gators were lovely creatures, easy to handle and perfect for letting nervous people get up close and personal. Neither of us could have wielded a crocodile like that, the way they thrash around. A croc will have you!

Alligators weren't harmless, of course. Nor was Stevo's hide impenetrable. And occasionally the jokes were on us.

At nesting time, the Fang sisters had a reputation for tearing into each other. Stevo or I would have to go in and grab them by their tails to pull them apart.

On one occasion I heard a crunch. Then, 'ohohoh'. Softly, though, because there were people watching.

A Fang sister had locked on to Stevo's hand. He considered it minor, I guess, but it would have felt like someone jumping on your fingers while wearing heavy boots.

'You're a good girl, let go now,' he whispered.

Before any of us hit the panic straps, she slowly opened her mouth and retreated into the water. On Stevo's injury severity scale, bruised fingers and a tooth mark probably rated 2 out of 10. Maybe on par with the time a 'harmless' boa constrictor bit his leg, drew blood and bruised his calf muscle black for weeks. The Fang sister's bite had power but she didn't try to tear his arm off. Not like Graham the saltie the following year…

*

With the park's burst of success came a burst of stress. Now that Stevo and I were officially work colleagues and in our late 20s, we felt the full weight of (Bob's) expectation. Sometimes we may have failed to show the required level of maturity.

Stevo sure didn't put on any airs and graces as the boss's son but he didn't mind issuing precise demands left, right and centre. Although just as headstrong, I generally acquiesced—mainly because he was usually right. Every now and then I'd arc up when feeling mischievous.

Chapter 11

Stevo and I get aggro over Agro. Bigger than the Big Pineapple. Thrifty not shifty. I almost lose an arm—but Stevo lends me a hand.

I was in an off mood one day when Stevo started complaining about the difficulties of mowing Agro's enclosure.

'Mate, I've come from a place where we had three and a half thousand crocodiles,' I said, referring to Hartley's Creek. 'You're whingeing about mowing one enclosure. It's not that hard, Steve.'

'Ohhh, you know, not too many people would be able to do it,' he said.

'That's bull, Steve. You've gotta realise, mate, that people who play with crocodiles are rare down here but in north Queensland plenty of them are doing it.'

That region had numerous crocodile farms, ranches and zoos, plus plenty of ex-croc shooters. Many residents literally lived with rogue crocs on their doorstep. I'd been responsible for handling and feeding 10 times the number of animals in Stevo's care at that time. Hartley's Creek even had a fantastic female croc wrangler, though it remained a blokey domain because the young guys saw it as a surefire way of pulling chicks.

Think about it. 'What do you do?' 'I catch deadly crocodiles.' Pretty suave.

So, to me, this was another day at the office.

'Well you mow Agro's enclosure,' he challenged.

No worries. I walked over and started pushing the machine.

He goaded me. 'Pretty hard isn't it?'

The reason everyone baulked at this enclosure was not because it had a particularly big or awkward lawn. It was the fact that Agro enjoyed launching himself at the lawnmower. That's 600 kilos (1300 pounds) of scaly croc body complete with his snapping jaws of death. Even if you got away unscathed, you wasted time constantly switching off the mower so Agro didn't cut his mouth on the blades and you could escape.

So I let Stevo in on my secret: a pocket full of pebbles with which to distract. Mow down to the water's edge and toss in a rock to find him. Wherever the rock hits the water you hear 'pssshhhhhh' as Agro zeroes in for an attack, thinking potential prey has broken the surface.

Wait for him to swim to that location and quickly use the opportunity to mow in the tight spots. Administer more pebbles as necessary. Alternate with banging on the ground to change his direction.

I'd learnt that the easy management of confined crocs relied on their predictability. They didn't weigh up an ambush. Agro wasn't thinking, 'If I manoeuvre that bloke into that corner I'll be able to chomp him.' The equation was way more primitive. Go to the water's edge, you're dead.

Time-efficiencies like this had been essential at Hartley's Creek. Another I demonstrated to Stevo was how to raid the females' nests for eggs. At Beerwah the common method was to catch the mother croc to tie her up or block her path with the backhoe bucket so she couldn't protect her eggs.

Instead, I used a broomstick to continually touch behind the female's back legs, making her spin around in stalk mode. As she tired, she stayed in one spot long enough for someone to remove the eggs.

I had to be very careful because some females would still charge the nest but this process was easier and less stressful to the animal than restraints. A top-jaw knot was only necessary if the female was in a really unsafe spot for the keeper.

With all of us learning and sharing knowledge, always moderated and modified by Bob, the park found a happy medium between a circus and conservation. It meant we were spreading the wildlife protection message, but also entertaining people, resulting in a wider audience.

Although Stevo was extremely enthusiastic about his work, he hadn't yet warmed to the public-speaking side of it. Bob certainly never spoke to the public. This was 1991. Very soon, Stevo would stun us by embracing the performance concept so heartily he became an Aussie legend.

*

Whitey remembers his amazement at the park's new direction. He compares it to his own early days of pumping out green, mossy water and hosing the freshwater crocodiles towards the fences so he could help Steve scrub the ponds. 'We did that on a regular basis and I always wondered why I turned my back to these critters who'd been pushed out of their territory,' Chris says. 'I was no reptile-handler and I never lost that uneasy feeling in those enclosures in the late 1970s and early '80s, particularly after Bob lost the partial use of one arm after a saltie grabbed him and deathrolled in shallow water. A bloke in the crowd reportedly jumped in to help save him.

'Ten years later it was incredible to see the change in the park, especially when Tony came back from Hartley's Creek and helped the Irwins kick off the interactive stuff with the public. Even though Bob hated the feeding shows at first and Tony could be pretty cocky, those shows were a catalyst for the park's success.

'Looking back, I think Tony and Steve were peas in a pod. Very similar temperaments and both with almost ADHD tendencies. Neither could sit still or chill out. Both had a temper and could fight quite handily.

Both had little fear (except Tony's hatred of needles).

'In fact, the only time I ever saw Steve panic was in Harriet's enclosure, of all places. It was a fine, sunny day in 1992, when Steve and I were 30 years old. My wife Mandy and I had taken our three-year-old daughter Karliah to visit the huge tortoise. Melinda had brought us a bucket of Harriet's favourite food—pawpaw, hibiscus flowers and broccoli stalks. A few of us were standing around chatting as we put Karliah over the barrier to feed Harriet. I had my back to her. Steve was facing her and Tony was beside him. I was talking to Steve when his face suddenly turned white. He belted past Tony and me and knocked Karliah out of the way.

'I'd thought of the tortoise as a gentle giant but she actually used her jaws as shears when chewing. Steve saw my toddler's hand too close to those jaws and knew she was about to lose a finger. Instead she lost a bit of blood when Harriet just nicked her. Steve, of course, was there in the nick of time.'

*

Yes, my time working at the park with Stevo was always eventful, but my favourite part of the day was twilight when I could just hang out with him in his incubator shed. As big as a double garage, it was made of old dark brown brick with a flat skillion tin roof and a side door near the Irwins' home.

Inside resembled a cross between Hannibal Lecter's toolshed and a maternity ward.

A ping pong table at one end was never used for that quaint sport. It was always covered in trigger mechanisms for traps, rifles, a spear gun modified as a croc harpoon, a crossbow and empty beer tallies. I'd spent many serious sessions around that ping pong table as Bob issued us with instructions and pointed to maps that he'd sketched while scouting out reptile territories up north.

Up against another wall were rolled-up croc nets of multiple colours and sizes. Surfboards, fishing rods and more spear guns were stacked on a half mezzanine floor.

Taking pride of place was an incubator fashioned from an old fridge. It was a relic—and Stevo wondered why some animals came out with curly tails instead of straight or with other mild deformities—but you couldn't knock it because it generally worked a treat. Depending on the time of year I'd see perentie lizard babies or the eggs of Burmese pythons, sand goannas or crocs.

When I'd worked at Hartley's Creek some people were quick to bag the Irwins and when Bob brought big crocodiles to the Sunshine Coast they said, 'He'll never breed 'em. It's too far south.'

Well, we bred 'em. Alligator snapping turtles, Reticulated pythons and the rest. Stick that in your pipe and smoke it.

In fact the Irwins hatched animals that no other zoo could. In the mid-1980s, the park crossbred the Proserpine rock wallaby with the Yellow-footed rock wallaby, producing not only fertile offspring, but also scientific proof that all wallabies came from one genus. Since both types were endangered, it was a coup for us, the Queensland Parks and Wildlife Service and the University of Queensland.

The Irwins succeeded with difficult-to-breed reptiles like tiger snakes, lace monitors and perenties, releasing endangered species back into the wild to boost their numbers. We believed the impact from humans and feral animals was devastating wildlife populations.

In the shed Stevo would be perched on his camp seat, fiddling, fussing or fixing something, and I would sit down next to him. Sometimes I'd still be there at 9 o'clock, having a beer and chatting about the day, family, friends, the future.

We listened to the comforting sounds outside: croc jaws slapping, alligators growling, whistling kites, the bloody peacocks going off. On one of those nights of reverie I remember saying to Stevo, 'One day, mate, this place will be bigger than the Big Pineapple. We'll get the people here.'

'You reckon Fris? I don't know. To be bigger than the Big Pineapple, wouldn't it be fantastic to have that many people?'

He probably thought I was riding the Nutmobile at the time. Named after the macadamia nut, that train was a feature of the Big Pineapple, a working pineapple plantation turned agricultural tourist attraction just up the highway at Nambour. Dominated by a 16-metre (52-foot) high coloured fibreglass replica of the spiky fruit, it was a huge hit with travellers and families from its opening in 1971.

Now, after years on the wane, the attraction has been eclipsed by Sunshine Coast competitors—namely Australia Zoo. In fact, the formerly humble reptile park has planned a $100 million expansion including an African safari and luxury hotel. It's expected to grow from 28 hectares (70 acres) to hundreds and its staff from 550 to 2000. Riper than a pineapple all right.

*

Such riches were unfathomable back in '91. Gate takings were rising nicely, adults were about $6 a head. But they didn't come close to covering the costs of upgrading infrastructure or the care, treatment and study of ever-increasing numbers of animals—let alone funding more than battered utes and baked beans on our 'bring 'em back alive' repeat trips up north and west.

I must say, though, that tinned food and unidentifiable camp oven concoctions never tasted so delicious as after the crap had been scared out of you by a Queensland predator.

Most things at the park operated on ingenuity—such as bartering with locals for goods and services—rather than cashflow. For example, we dug out new ponds and boxed up new pathways, all ready for infill, then worried how we could afford the concrete.

Someone made an arrangement with a concrete mixing company to use their leftovers on their way back from jobs. I'm pretty sure the 'arrangement' involved a carton of grog.

So the driver would phone Lyn on the front counter to say he had .2 or .4 in the truck and to get ready. I'd hear Lyn on the PA system: 'Concrete's arriving, concrete's arriving, point four of a metre, Tony can you open the side gate?'

I'd open the gate and 10 minutes later the truck would be directed to the enclosures for the pour. Sweet. The key was to be prepared for the concrete whenever available or it got dumped.

If we needed shaped rocks for landscaping, Stevo and I would go out into the bush or roadwork cuttings after the gates at the zoo had closed for the day and get some. On one outing we sweated buckets trying to lift a rock easily weighing a tonne and a half on to the ute. It was frustrating, but we managed to roll it on to boards, shuffle it along and use a Tirfor winch to get it up on the trayback.

When we returned we needed a backhoe to pull it off. I needed a nice lie-down.

*

One day the park got an ominous call. Someone had seen a crocodile in a private dam at Landsborough. At first we assumed it was a bad joke or a prank, not the first ever played on us. Then we guessed mistaken identity. It was probably a goanna swimming across the water. Crocodiles didn't live this far south.

But Stevo and I were uneasy about the 'what ifs'. What if it was an escapee from our park? What if it bit a cow—or a kid? What if someone called the authorities and it was a croc and they shot it unnecessarily? We decided to do some secret investigating. Little did I know that I would be its bloodied victim and Stevo would have to save me.

That night he picked me up because my house was only 10 minutes' drive from the suspect dam. He had the tinnie on the back of his truck, just in case. We pulled up beside the dam with a torch, opened the bonnet to connect the spotlight and waved it over the dam. Bloody hell. There *was* an eye-shine in there. All systems go.

We put the boat in the shallows, piled in the gear and out we went. Our actions were based on careful speculation in the truck cabin en route. There were only two theories.

First, someone had brought a baby down from Cape York, reared it and let it go. That sounded like an urban myth, even to our ears. Second, it was one of our zoo animals. That wasn't physically impossible because waterways were linked in the region and our grounds had flooded before.

If that was correct we had to catch it without fail.

We motored towards the eye-shine, slowly, cautiously, but it submerged rapidly. We went out a second time, closer, closer. Nope, it pulled under again.

'We're not gonna get real close to this one Stevo,' I worried.

'We'll keep working it, keep working it,' he said.

I told him I thought I could take a shot at it. By shot, I meant jump. So I jumped. As I latched on to the thick base of its tail—not the best place to grab a croc—it spun around and bit my arm, near my wrist, and starting dropping under the water.

With one hand stuck in its mouth while hanging on to its tail, my other hand gripped its neck. It was only about 4 feet (1.2 metres), but it was locked on my forearm and biting deeper.

I could no longer tread water and went under.

Suddenly Stevo's giant hand reached down and hooked me by the scruff of the neck. He reefed me over to the side of the boat. How he didn't flip the tinnie, I don't know. He was trying to hold both me and crocodile above water.

I yelled, 'It's got me! It's got me!'

'You've got it, you've got it,' he laughed, outwardly cool as a cucumber. He grabbed the croc and said, 'Let it go.'

I refused.

Now he yelled. 'Mate, if you let it go, it'll let you go!'

I wasn't being tough or a martyr, I thought it would start twisting. When a croc twists, it can take a heap of skin and flesh off you.

At some point, Stevo hauled the croc into the boat and I released my grip. As soon as I did, it let me go. He was right. And we had caught it.

I scrambled back in the boat and we made our sorry way home. I walked in dripping blood as Melinda said, 'What's happened to you?' She was pretty casual about it—such incidents were part and parcel of our lives back then. A couple of beers fixed us.

For about three weeks I couldn't jump any fences or put weight on that unbelievably sore arm. The teeth had gone right through to scratch the bone.

Oh yeah, we never found out where the croc was from. It was a juvenile so no use checking for scute cuts, which were identification marks we only put on adult crocs at the park. Notch it up to experience.

Chapter 12

Man or mouse? Stevo: 'I'll grab the head end'. Melinda's slant on team Irwin-Frisby. Taking work home. 'Man talk' about a new woman.

Knowing how tough Stevo was, would you believe a mouse was once his undoing?

We were all hard at it one day when he disappeared into the park's mouse house. This exhibit was in the middle of a concrete building that also had one male toilet, one female toilet and a tiny basin.

The park needed to provide more toilets but the mouse house stank. Sometimes when the humidity was high, you'd walk in and your eyes watered at all the rodent droppings. Stevo made it his pet project to move the mice and renovate it into a modern amenities block.

Crash! Whack! A couple of hours later I heard almighty hell in there. Stevo lost the plot. Something didn't fit. I think it was a timber join because he had been building a beautiful wooden change bench for mothers with babies.

Instead he took the sledgehammer to the inside of the toilet block, accompanied by choice words. Walls crumbled. Afterwards, not a thing was left in that concrete building.

When he eventually stormed out I turned to Melinda and said, 'Hmm, stay away from there.'

It was for the best. Few people ever saw Stevo's bad temper—and that was lucky for them.

*

Melinda left her job at a Beerwah pharmacy to join the park in August 1991 as a third curator and administrative assistant. She handled birds and helped at the front counter and food outlet. She also had known the Irwins since her teens and appreciated their quirks and compassion as much as I did.

My wife loved looking after Harriet the giant Galapagos tortoise. Beerwah's only specimen of this endangered species had been brought back from Fleay's Fauna Sanctuary on the Gold Coast when it was under redevelopment in 1987. She was the size of a dinner table.

Harriet was a darling and Melinda and I often rubbed oil into her shell and legs to stop them cracking. You'd have dry skin too if you were more than a century and a half old.

Stevo was also devoted to gentle Harriet, who died aged 175 in June 2006—just months before his own sudden death. Harriet's 15 November birthday has since been turned into the annual Steve Irwin Day. In 2007 the inaugural event drew 6000 people to the zoo.

Melinda even got game enough to jump in the deep end with me and Stevo.

She recalls:

'By 1991 Tony had been doing all these things with Steve so I went up to Cattle Creek too. When they did this jumping on crocs I was gobsmacked. I loved the whole idea of it.

'Steve had more experience but Tony was a really quick learner and very good with animals so it just was natural to see them doing these things.

'I was never scared for them because I knew they would do exactly what they said. They would jump on that croc in the water and they would come back up. They would put it in the boat and we would go on.

'It never occurred to me that they couldn't do something because they were very confident people.

'I enjoyed watching Tony and Steve together, they were a great combination. They had to be really precise. It wasn't just jumping on a crocodile, there was so much involved.

'At times I held the spotlight. I'd be thinking, "I hope I'm doing the right thing," because any slight move could put their lives at risk. So I was careful. I didn't let the spotlight waver.'

Melinda says she enjoyed the constant surprises in her job description at the park. And like any loving wife, she can't resist a dig.

'I remember when Steve wanted to move the park's big Reticulated python to another enclosure. He walked past his mum Lyn and me, motioned for us to help and simply said, "I'll grab the head end."

'We thought the three of us could carry this 22-foot (6.5-metre) snake but we needed a fourth person. Tony came by. "I'm not dragging that thing," he said.

'This snake used to eat goats. It was very heavy and strong. If it started to move you really had to hold on because if it got one coil around Steve or any of us, we would be squashed. There would be no way to get it off.

'Tony eventually conceded on the proviso, "I'm only taking the back end." We all laughed.

'It didn't bother me. Whenever Steve said to grab something, that's what I did. I never thought twice about it. If Steve or Tony told me to stand in a croc enclosure, for example, that's what I did. I never got hurt. That's the trust that I and other staff had in both of them. I can't say I'd do it with anyone else.

'Now, even with Tony today, if we're diving or doing something risky, I listen to every word he says. Don't muck around, don't ask questions.

'Those two knew what they were talking about. They never made things up to sound dramatic or look good. There was a safety reason for it. They were a great couple of years.'

*

Melinda was spot-on about our reliance on trust and communication. Every time Stevo and I trapped a cranky croc, our lives were at stake. When one of us leapt on the bitey end to cover the eyes, the croc quickly judged our weight. The first thing he did was swing. If you were thrown off, the second thing he did was bite.

Stevo and I relied on each other to either stop the swing—or the bite.

These trips were much more than fun adventures. They saved the lives of some fantastic old crocs (possibly saving human lives too—or at least helping communities feel safer), replenished reptile numbers at the park and boosted research on reptile species and habits in conjunction with universities, the Queensland Museum and government departments.

On a personal level they laid the foundations for Stevo's wildlife career and also set me on a path of raising awareness about conservation through to my current job as a Parks and Wildlife ranger in north Queensland. I still get great pleasure in describing to people how animals work, dispelling myths about crocs, rather than leaving education completely to static displays and books.

I absorbed everything Stevo showed me, whether it involved man-eaters or insects. On one of our Cape York jaunts in the late '80s to look for mangrove monitors, we had driven past an eye-catching termite mound topping 7 metres (23 feet).

'Get a look at that hole in the top,' Stevo said. 'Someone's shot the top out of it.' He told me to stand on the truck to show the dimensions for this photograph (colour pages vi). I wondered why it angered him so much.

I later referred to that incident in zoo talks, to illustrate the environmental impact of idiotic things like shooting holes in harmless termite mounds. As Stevo explained to me, the grass-eating termites (enemy of the meat ants) take years to build these intricate structures which regulate the temperature of the colony at 30 degrees Celsius (86 degrees Fahrenheit).

The conical mounds become home to many other tropical species from goannas to birds, including kingfishers and the endangered Golden-shouldered parrot. Because the mound's climate control can only safely fluctuate a few tenths of a degree, gouging out any part of it breaks down the whole ecosystem. The termites terminate their community, letting their eggs die.

*

Back at Beerwah, our little community braced for its own fluctuations.

A filmmaker and television producer named John Stainton, who regularly visited the park to get footage of animals for TV commercials, had been bowled over by Stevo's pile of home movies. They reminded me of a manic Harry Butler from *In The Wild*, a popular Aussie bush series on TV in the '70s and '80s.

Bob had given his only son the video camera to record his solo croc escapades for family and friends. Stevo, of course, had taken it to the extreme. He taped hours and hours of his craziness, tying the camera to a tree branch or the car if he couldn't balance the tripod.

When the two of us were catching crocs around Camp Chilli I helped with videoing, but even I would end up leaving the camera perched precariously on the bullbar. Let's face it, when you're pushing feisty crocs into boxes it's all hands on deck—spend too long checking a camera angle and you may lose a limb!

John Stainton was impressed with Stevo's screen presence and courage. John had lots of TV contacts and started planning a documentary series. Behind all the lenses, a marketing machine started to whir.

Melinda and I were settling into a new property in the Glass House

Mountains behind Beerwah. We had bought 2.5 lush hectares (6 acres) from Bob and Lyn.

We were living in a shed, but felt like we were saving the world, both at work and home. The Irwin fever had got us, and we started caring for flora and fauna 24/7. The ambition was fine, but we gave ourselves heartaches.

A lot of injured fauna was being brought into the park at the time, as the development of the Sunshine Coast started encroaching on the coastal and hinterland environments.

Achieving a balance between urban development and environmental protection remains one of the Coast's biggest issues, as it passes a population of 300,000. Little wonder the Australian Wildlife Hospital at the zoo is still so busy. Wildlife Warriors Worldwide, the group started by Stevo, recently reported the wildlife hospital was getting 100 emergency calls a day, with 70 percent of admitted animals the victims of car accidents or domestic pet attacks.

At first Melinda and I tried to save every animal, whereas Lyn would look at particular injuries and just say, 'No, we'll have to euthanase it.' I fought this powerlessness but, as always with Irwin education, I eventually learnt when to act and when to spare my emotions.

I took home a beautiful Crested hawk that had been swiped by a car.

'Nah, it's not gonna make it,' Stevo told me. Despite his judgement and Lyn's knowledge, I was determined to nurse it. Four or five days went by and I was pretty proud of my efforts.

'It took two mice last night,' I reported to Stevo in delight.

The next morning it was dead. Apparently a slow-acting infection had set in. That was a tough lesson, and I guess they knew I had to learn the hard way.

Melinda's turn came with a Feathertail glider which she nestled in my grandmother's old wooden cupboard in our shed home. Gliders are tiny, like flying mice.

Lyn had told us, 'I don't think it'll survive, but you can give it a go.'

The little beggar made it. Late one cold afternoon we walked up a hill overlooking five of the craggy Glass House Mountains and put the glider on a tree branch. It scurried up the trunk as we smiled goodbye.

A kookaburra flew straight for it and whack! Ate it.

I was shattered. We had nursed it for nine months. We should have waited until it was darker, after the kookas had settled down.

We learnt from our mistakes and had wonderful successes. The park received a lot of Tawny frogmouths, nocturnal owl-like birds that would get hit by cars while hunting insects in the headlights. They're cuties, with fluffy mottled grey feathers and less than 50-centimetres (20-inches) long.

We got a baby named Gobbie when he was a day old. A ball of fluff—all body with a little curious face. Gobbie lived in an icecream container until he could fly and then he lived on top of the cupboard. We fed him at night and he loved the legs off day-old chickens.

When we got home from the park each day, we would throw open the shed door and bolt inside to find Gobbie, grab him and put him outside on the ground. His poos were huge and horrible and if he dropped one inside we'd never get rid of the smell. He became part of our family.

Every time I started to consider myself 'experienced', Stevo would show me something new. One day he came over to see our home collection and I said, 'Mate, I think one of my snakes is crook.'

He scooped her up, glanced and suddenly dropped her.

'Careful! What are you doing?' I said.

'Mites. She's got mites, that's why she's not feeding,' he diagnosed. He rushed to the sink and washed his arms thoroughly to avoid passing on any infestation. Like fleas on dogs, mites can be impossibly hard to eradicate and do untold damage at zoos. But these were so tiny I couldn't even see them.

'Put pest strips in the container, mate. Get rid of those mites.'

So I did. My snakes regained their health.

If only I'd been this willing to follow orders at the park, I might have avoided the bloody big trauma to come.

*

One hot day in October 1991 I was in the glass snake enclosure feeding a dead chook to the giant Reticulated python. Steve G was on the opposite side feeding the Burmese python and smaller, motley-coloured corn snakes. About 10 people were gathered in front of me.

Back then we didn't do snake shows as such, we just fed our reptiles and answered questions like, 'Is it venomous?'

No, pythons use constriction.

'Why do you feed them mice?'

Right size, available, tasty.

'What's reticulated mean?'

It refers to the diamond pattern on their scales.

There were four locked glass enclosures in that block surrounded by a welded mesh external enclosure with steel gates. We had many highly venomous natives and highly prized exotic species. In the cool of the night we rolled down canvas covers and switched on lights to help the glass retain heat. Snakes love warmth.

The python weighed about 100 kilograms (220 pounds) so I was focused on my task. Until I noticed a buxom long-haired brunette and her equally attractive blonde short-haired friend pressing against the glass to get a closer look.

Happily married, I liked to point out potential girlfriends to my unlucky-in-love 29-year-old mate Stevo. I knew he was on the hunt and I knew these two ladies were a rarity among the park's normal demographic of families and elderly couples soaking up the tranquility. Not to mention the bikie tours.

And it wasn't just their looks. Other chicks screwed up their faces or said 'ewwww' when they walked past the snakes, but these two seemed genuinely interested.

While the python consumed its meal, I slipped out of the enclosure, looped the padlock through the gate and bolted to where Stevo was having smoko with his old man under a tree.

'Hey Stevo! Fair sort at the snakes.'

'Yeah, yeah, sure Fris.'

'Serious. There's an opportunity here mate, okay?' I laughed and rushed back to my work.

Stevo did walk past, on his way to join me for the 3 o'clock crocodile and alligator feed. It wasn't great timing—he was sweaty and would have smelled like the fowl he'd just prepared in extreme humidity for the feed. He was wearing one of our khaki button-up work shirts and dark blue Stubbies. Probably barefoot.

'Ohhh. That's all right,' he nodded after getting an eyeful of the ladies.

We gave a brief talk to a small crowd, bouncing anecdotes and information off each other, while Stevo fed Monty the saltie. We explained that Stevo would be presenting the next show over in the Crocodile Environmental Park in 10 minutes. People rushed to buy tickets.

Including the attractive duo.

Next time our paths crossed, Stevo was telling me about meeting the brunette after his show. I was totally impressed. She was a 27-year-old holidaymaker from Oregon and she seemed real interested in what he had to say. Her name was Terri Raines.

*

Their romance was rapid and initially I loved the fact that he had fallen head over heels, finally. Terri spent that first weekend hanging out with the Irwins at the park and sightseeing. Stevo was showing off, as you do. They traded stories of rehabilitating Aussie and American predators. Steve: crocs. Terri: cougars.

I suspected Stevo was a little rusty at courting when he plonked her in the Glasshouse Mountains Motel overnight instead of trying it on. He'd been up north by himself and in one of his dry spells, as we had discussed in our usual obnoxious blokey way.

He and Terri went out to tea at a restaurant in Caloundra and he politely ended the date. But later he raved to me: 'Oh I just can't wait to see her again! I'm going nuts.' Terri also later revealed she had wished for a goodnight kiss. Oh, Stevo!

They did a back-and-forth thing across the globe, visiting each other. He took Terri to the Burdekin and immersed her in park life. In between we weren't getting much work out of him. He was over the moon, the happiest I'd seen him in a long time.

We thought Terri was warm, friendly and driven. Unlike Stevo's previous girlfriends, Terri shared his obsessions. She talked passionately about her own work protecting the cougars, bobcats, raccoons and other wildlife. She had her own facility called Cougar Country.

Even their differences somehow suited: Aussie versus Yank accents; her careful planning versus the method in his madness. She looked refined, airbrushed. He was simply unbrushed. So opposite yet so much in common. We thought they were meant to be together.

Chapter 13

Engaged already! Stevo tries performance art, croc style. Build and they will come. First bite of fame ends in blood.

Only months later Stevo floored me. We were at the wedge-tail eagle enclosure looking into the black snake enclosure and he said, 'What do you think about me asking Terri to marry me?'

'You're kiddin' aren't ya?' I replied.

'No. Whaddya reckon Fris?'

Well. Mr I-Only-Love-My-Dog-And-Crocs wanted to pop the question. I thought hard.

'Mate, yeah. She seems like a really nice chick. You've got a lot in common and that.'

He smiled, excited. 'So how was it when you and Mins (Melinda) got engaged?'

I offered my wisdom as a hubby of, oh, a couple of years and we had a longer discussion about married life. He repeated, 'So whaddya think?'

'Mate, you'll have to ask her.'

That's the way it was with our group of guys. If I was going to do something important, I'd ask Stevo or Rod or Mick for their opinion. And vice versa. None of us was ever short of a no-bull comment.

After Terri said yes in February 1992, she returned to the States to prepare for her move to the Sunshine Coast and their wedding in Oregon on 4 June.

At some point Stevo asked me to be his best man. I was honoured because it showed how much he respected our friendship. Obviously the feeling was mutual. Stevo had been one of my groomsmen in '89. But it seemed natural rather than a big deal. All of us boys preferred talking about the rude stuff of relationships rather than wedding dates, venues or traditions. Stevo knew Terri would do a much better job with all the practical stuff, anyway.

Things started moving ridiculously fast then—both at the ever-growing park and in our changing personal lives. Still, I never guessed that by the end of '92, my mate and his new American wife would be running the future Australia Zoo and mullet-cropped Stevo would be starring in the first episode of *The Crocodile Hunter* documentary TV series.

And Hollywood lay in wait.

Meanwhile Bob and Lyn bought a property at Rosedale, about 330 kilometres (200 miles) north of Beerwah near Bundaberg on the east coast, with the intention of growing palm trees to sell to developers. Palms were very fashionable in new housing estates and the Irwins figured it would make a decent income to help support the wildlife park.

They were preparing to set up residence at Rosedale and hand management of the park to their capable, willing son and his bride.

I will never forget Bob saying to me, 'Look after Steve.'

*

Swelling waves of visitors started threatening to swamp our park. Bob, Stevo and I realised we could no longer house them all at the normal exhibits.

Stevo had decided to build a stand near the general crocodile enclosures. 'It'll hold 200 people, Fris, it'll be massive!'

We built it all right, but within months the stand had outgrown itself. More and more people seemed obsessed with crocodiles. Fancy that.

But the Crocodile Environmental Park really hit its straps when we introduced the vertical attack show. Stevo and I debated the concept in great detail before agreeing on the construction of a feeding platform so the crowds could see crocs leaping from the water for food. He must have approved—he later designed it into the current high-tech Crocoseum.

First Stevo had to be sure it straddled the fine line between education to boost conservation and entertainment to boost attendance figures. He refused point blank to come at the idea of a death roll show like I did at Hartley's Creek, fearing harm to the animals. But we had both witnessed vertical attacks as regular behaviour in the wild, when crocs went after birds, bats, anything on low mangrove branches or anything tall at the water's edge.

It was a pretty important thing to show tourists who might venture into Queensland's croc-infested north, too. Most of this state's fatal attacks have involved campers, swimmers and fishermen in remote areas who don't know or ignore the dangers.

Sadly, as I write this chapter in February 2009, the far north is mourning two deaths. A five-year-old boy taken by a croc in a creek near his Daintree home, and a man in his 60s taken near Cooktown after checking on crab pots at a river bank. As horrendous as these tragedies are, they're not common. The death toll from croc attacks in Queensland is now seven in 23 years. That's why ongoing research and management is so vital.

So Stevo and I built this wooden deck with a steel frame about 2.5 metres (8 feet) above a muddy pond at the entrance to the Crocodile Environmental Park. Anvil, a very old, 4-metre (13-foot) saltie, was our inaugural star.

Anvil had a scissor jaw and few teeth and had lived for decades in a concrete pond in an original enclosure. Stevo and I were delighted to move him from beside Monty to the spacious mud enclosure under the new deck.

The next process was simple. I walked to the deck's edge, held out a chook and pleaded, 'C'mon Anvil.'

Anvil rose and submerged in the 2.5 metre (8 feet) deep water, judging the situation. I saw the points on his snout before he disappeared again.

'C'mon Anvil.'

Roar! He shot vertically, using his powerful tail for leverage to get half his body out of the water.

Smack! Unfortunately he focused on my legs instead of the chicken and hit his head on the angled steel support bolted just under my feet.

Not good. Plan B. How to teach him the right approach? Impossible to change a croc's mind, of course. We spent days redesigning the ramp so we could lean out further, redirecting Anvil's efforts to the feathers

Our first star: Anvil the saltie leaps from the water at the Beerwah reptile park. This was one of the first croc performances that Tony introduced with Stevo in the early 1990s.

Success. The vertical attack demo was instantly one of the park's main drawcards. Amateurs and professionals came to film it. Anvil even started waiting at the fenceline, spinning around when he saw the chook, to the crowd's delight.

When the crowds were gone, I remember just standing there with Stevo as we watched Anvil revel in his new pond, coating himself in mud. We congratulated ourselves for getting the old beast back in his element. Anvil even started growing new teeth after we changed his diet.

You can't trust nature. Anvil

died within a year of his move. At least he had that year.

As we perfected the technique with different crocs and got great reactions, Stevo began to understand the rewards of performance. The punishments would be more painful.

*

I could not have imagined a more ironic disaster than what happened when a Channel 10 News crew set up in our Crocodile Environmental Park to tape Graham being moved in 1992.

It started with a belligerent croc, escalated to Stevo being pulled from the pond with a hole that you could see through in his palm, and finished with his sister Mandy taking him to hospital.

Further proof, I guess, of two Irwin traits I was all too familiar with. First, mind over matter for physical pain. Second, if at first you don't succeed, don't stop 'til you drop.

In those days we were slowly getting used to TV crews and the occasional celebrity, such as the ever-smiling Jackie MacDonald, who we recognised from popular variety show *Hey, Hey, It's Saturday* and who instantly got on well with Stevo. Producer John Stainton always had a project on the go, and later came Channel 10's children's program *Totally Wild*.

On this occasion at the enclosure of sub-adult crocodiles, none of us guessed an accident would help kick-start Stevo's TV notoriety. Most of the crocs in this enclosure were between one and two metres long, but Graham was a bit older and pushing 2.5 metres (8 feet). He was bulkier than the others and had started biting their tails, damaging them. Most males became territorial when they reached sexual maturity at over 3 metres (almost 10 feet). So he had to be moved.

My first surprise was seeing Stevo tuck in his khaki workshirt. He really was trying to blend into this shiny new role. We all stood guard on the water's edge after the crew had set up their gear—cameras, mikes, lights, the whole bit.

Stevo banged on a white bucket to entice Graham, who sat pleasantly in the water.

We could only see his sly head.

Repeated attempts failed. 'Twas not to be.

Between all the hoop-la and the juvenile crocs wandering around, there was no way Graham would play ball.

Stevo apologised over and over. He was ropable. Our VIP visitors departed for the day.

'Righteo.' Stevo's brain whirred. 'Next time we'll get smarter. We'll position the camera over here so Graham doesn't know what's going on. We'll make no fuss. No one goes anywhere near that enclosure until I say.'

When the cameraman came back, I asked Stevo if he wanted me to try enticing Graham towards the new enclosure. I'd been regularly feeding this feisty reptile and hoped that might have a positive effect. I knew Stevo was antsy about making sure the TV professionals got the shot they wanted. And at that time they didn't yet care which keeper, as long as the croc was in focus.

'Nah nah, I'll get it,' Stevo said. After all, he had single-handedly brought Graham back from Townsville in 1988.

'Okay, but just concentrate on what's going on there,' I said, holding the bucket. 'Don't worry about the camera, he'll get what's needed.'

Stevo agreed, but he was extra-hypo from nerves. He'd combed his hair, done up his shirt and was wearing a pair of shorts that didn't have the butt ripped out of them.

I stood to one side. The TV guy started filming alone, just with his camera on his shoulder. Minimum fuss. He zeroed in on Stevo, half-crouched by the water's edge.

Graham stuck up his head. Stevo called him. Graham started coming out of the water.

Showing more confidence, Stevo kept chatting while doing the feed.

'Looks like he's gonna come, you right? You got it?' he said.

The croc baulked.

He planted his short, stocky, front legs on the water's edge and stopped. (Graham, that is—though Stevo's stocky legs were also planted firmly.)

Stevo frantically waved the dead chook. 'C'mon matey, c'mon now.'

In one hand was the top-jaw rope (lasso), in the other the chicken. 'C'mon Graham!'

Stevo got the croc up close and prepared to throw the noose.

Bite! Bite! Graham did a double whammy. He grabbed the chook, but had a second go, clamping on Stevo's right hand by mistake.

Within seconds, my mate was getting dragged into the water. There were 23 crocs in that enclosure. Most of them have 64 teeth.

I jumped the fence, sprinted across and yelled, 'you right, mate?' as we pulled him out. Racing through my head were two thoughts: 'Oh no, this guy's getting married,' and then 'Bob's gonna kill me.'

Thankfully, Graham's jaw had released after they hit the water. Stevo later explained that he knew if he wrenched back his hand, Graham would have ripped it off. So he fell forward with the croc, actually landing on top of Graham in the water.

That finally got a smile out of me. Graham would have freaked. He wouldn't have expected a 90-kilogram human deadweight instead of a delicious chicken morsel.

'Are you right?' I wasn't convinced.

'Yeah I'm right. Damn! We didn't get it. Sorry guys, sorry, sorry, it didn't work.'

Amid the fuss, Stevo just kept apologising. He didn't mention his injury. He was filthy mad that the cameraman didn't get what they'd planned. He hated disappointing people, especially when he'd made a business commitment.

But I saw his hand—that big beefy palm had a coin-sized hole clean through the middle and more punctures extending out to the edge of his pinky. It looked white. Technically I knew he had sustained a concentrated force many times greater than a sledgehammer. Mentally I remembered the extent of my pain after a much lesser bite on my arm in that dam.

I said 'Let's go,' and unlocked the environmental park gate for them. Stevo walked over to Melinda at the front counter. She recalls:

'I'll never forget that because it was quite funny. Steve walked casually up and I said, "What are you doing here?" He had his hand on his head. I thought he might be joking around. But no, he just told me calmly what happened. Anybody else would have been screaming!'

While Mandy took her brother to hospital, we all sat down to discuss the footage. Of course the TV people were on the phones immediately. It was 4pm. Far from disappointed, they wanted the drama to make the prime time news that evening. It wasn't every day the public could witness a saltwater crocodile attack in south-east Queensland.

We asked them—very politely—not to release it yet. By smoko we had reached an agreement that they wouldn't screen it until we had contacted Bob and Lyn at Rosedale. Pretty accommodating of them, really.

When the scene aired, the Steve Irwin legend got another boost. He was definitely in the public eye. His parents came down to check on him but, as usual, he wasn't scared off. We all noticed the park's newfound popularity that weekend. You should have seen the number of people through the gate. I heard one lady at a show tell her partner, 'Get this on video, honey, this guy's gonna get eaten.'

People don't go to speedways to watch cars drive around. They go to see crashes. People don't go to the footy to watch a ball thrown around. They want to see guys smash themselves. So it was a no-brainer to see so many people at our crocodile shows. It was up to us to work out how to use human nature to benefit wildlife as well.

The intrepid cameraman Shane Dyson, who now heads Channel 10's Brisbane production unit, remembers being surprised at both the amount of blood and the lack of panic that afternoon. 'I'd been sent there, without a journo, to get stock footage of this croc,' he recalls. 'I'd met Steve a few times before but in those days he was just Bob Irwin's son. I said g'day and he said he'd get some shots for me.'

Shane says arrangements were very casual. 'We just jumped the fence into the pen and I couldn't see anything below the pond's surface. It was nowhere near as sophisticated as the zoo is now. Steve said, "all right, we'll get this croc out for ya" and out it came.

'I don't know whether Steve got too close with the chicken or the croc over-lunged, but its big tooth went right through his hand and dragged him back into the water. If you're a cameraman you just go with what's happening and somehow I also ended up in there, wet to my thighs. It happened so quick, a few seconds.

All Steve said was, "Oh he's got me," and in he went. I don't know why, but the croc let him go. There was blood everywhere.'

Shane says Steve's minimal reaction to the injury, even while they walked to the office to call for medical help, made the incident seem funny. 'His arm wasn't ripped off, he wasn't bleeding to death from an artery, he *only* had a puncture. And I had great pictures, thank you very much!

'It only shocked me later, when Steve said he was glad the croc didn't do a death roll or it would have finished him. I didn't have that sort of knowledge, I knew people could get taken by crocs but I didn't think by the hand.'

A cameraman for 28 years on programs such as *Totally Wild*, Shane's had many more jobs at the zoo and says he never felt in danger because of the staff's expertise, particularly Steve's. 'If they tell you to stand somewhere, you know you'll be right. Steve was a nice, down-to-earth bloke, another keeper who was easy to work with. He was so good at being himself in front of the camera. I always had confidence that he really knew a creature. It was in the way he spoke, his mannerisms, the way he conducted himself around it. Steve was special but we couldn't have the same working relationship when he became the megastar. He'd get mobbed too often.'

As for Graham? A couple of weeks later I walked in there with the same noose for his top jaw and Stevo and I got him out, no worries. And no cameras.

Today Graham is known as the zoo's most notorious croc, as he grows nearer to 4 metres (13 feet). It's thought he never forgave Stevo for relocating him from that Townsville boat ramp surrounded by tasty fishermen's castoffs.

Years later, during a stormy night in 2001, Graham cemented his infamy by latching on to Wes Mannion's bum and thigh when he and Stevo were trying to reinforce the fences. I heard the bite was nasty. A lot of stitches.

*

Despite my rough 'n' tumble life of boxing and footy, I never met anyone with a higher pain threshold than Stevo. He brushed aside every mishap. He was full of scars from daily work, but he was hard. His finger was broken in two places but he never bothered to get it treated.

As for that videotape showing his refusal to accept the injury to his leg after the Joan Collins chomp...we weren't the only ones left shaking our heads. I believe John Stainton did the same and when more of Stevo's shenanigans aired in his first Channel 10 doco in 1992, I reckon most of Queensland did too.

Stevo had crawled inside the capture box, leading Joan by a top jaw rope like some sort of 2.7 metre-long pet dog. Once a rope lasso was in position around a croc's teeth and the bulbous part of the snout there was no chance of it coming loose. So Joan followed all right.

Snap! She bit clean through Stevo's leather boots and took chunks of flesh before letting go. He kept working, barely acknowledging the bloody holes. He got this nine-footer in the box, processed her and arranged for transportation before checking his own limbs.

Jibba, who also did a lot of surfing and spear fishing with Stevo on the Sunshine Coast, remembers that Stevo 'always had broken toes and blood coming out of him'. Jibba continues:

'Even back in high school, Steve was always showing us his injuries. "See where I came off me skateboard? Check out this fin chop. Look, a goanna bit me here." We'd say sarcastically, "Yeah, righto, you're a winner."'

Jibba and Chris recall a shocking injury Steve copped when he was a young teenager. Chris says, 'There was a sizeable shorebreak at Moffat Beach. Big sucky waves. We loved it but Steve, who was still learning, was getting crunched up. Still, he refused to come in when we did. A couple of us were showering when I saw him coming up over the rocks. "What happened?" we asked. "Ah I got fin-chopped." His bicep was sliced deep. The muscle actually popped out.

'No one had a mobile phone or money so we went up to the local shop. The attendant Michelle, who was in my older sister's class, said, "What have you done?" Steve slowly put his elbow on the curved glass of the stainless steel refrigeration cabinet. The whole muscle fell out. There was very little blood. The girl freaked. Steve ended up with 52 stitches, internal and external, with a thick scar.'

Jibba recalls Steve's dangerous method of spear-fishing. 'For whatever reason he hated the rope on his spear gun. "Ah, bloody thing gets in the road, I'm just getting rid of it." Then he'd spear mangrove jack off the Kings Beach headland and because he had no rope to retrieve them, we'd see him disappear into holes in the rock, going after the wounded fish. He'd always reappear with them, though.

'Once, though, at Wurtulla rocks, he speared a bream and pushed his hand at the sharpened prongs to stop it coming loose. A prong stabbed the base of his little finger and busted out the tip. Straight through. I was pretty shocked, especially considering how rusted our guns were. Steve had no intention of seeing a doctor. A couple of us unscrewed the prong end from the handle and took Steve back to Toomsy's place at Currimundi.

'Toomsy put it in a vice—with Steve still attached and bleeding—then simply cut it off and pulled it out. No anaesthetic. "I'll be right," Steve told us, "I had a tetanus shot for something else last week." I think he used Band-Aids and Dettol and a few weeks later it was healing okay.'

Chapter 14

Irwins in Oregon: from cordial beer to cougars. Burritos with Stevo's in-laws. Weddings, parties, everything. Zoo envy.

Bob and Lyn went through a terrible time at Rosedale. The tree business proved expensive in set-up costs (established palms cost a pretty penny) then they lost everything when heavy rains caused major flooding between Caloundra and Gladstone.

But they were determined to make a go of it. Stevo went up to help the clean-up. Still wielding his injured Graham hand, he lifted and transported healthy palms back to the park from Rosedale while Bob and Lyn made plans to rebuild the house on higher ground.

It reinforced Stevo's desire to make the park a financial success to help his parents overcome their hardships.

I don't think any of us fully realised the power of the media until 1992. How it could make business boom in the blink of a camera's eye. In the Aussie TV landscape at the time, there was a hole where Paul Hogan's *Crocodile Dundee* had left off and real-life bush adventurers were ageing. And here was Stevo. Young, smart and full of daring. John Stainton provided him with the opportunity and Terri, the commercial nous.

There was no turning back.

As 4 June neared, Melinda and I worried about travelling to America for the big white wedding. Melinda was matron of honour and felt as privileged as me to be in the wedding party. I'd only been best man once before, at my mate Clive's wedding. But I had warned Stevo at the outset we weren't sure if we could afford it. All the festivities were being held in the States, including bucks' and hens' nights. We knew it was going to be a fancy do with a crowd of guests.

We were still living in our rural shed. I was using my brickie skills to fix things up. I'd been in partnership with Mick for years previously, building houses around Maroochydore and Kawana, but the housing industry wasn't the gold mine it is now on the Sunshine Coast.

Melinda and I didn't have kids yet, but our park wages weren't luxurious. To be honest, we were on the seat of our pants.

Stevo came up to me one day looking serious. 'Look mate, I'll give you some money to help you guys get over there.'

I refused, embarrassed. By hook or by crook, we would be on that plane.

Stevo and Terri's wedding trip to Oregon. After the big event we went on a road trip in a minivan to see the sights. (L-R) Mick, Melinda, Lyn with granddaughter Rebecca, Stevo, Terri and Terri's mum Julia.

Chapter 14

America was a whole new adventure for our group of mates. Seven of Stevo's family and friends spent almost a fortnight in La-La land. We made a distinct Aussie impression on Eugene, Oregon after flying in from Los Angeles.

Bob and Lyn joined the Aussie wedding party contingent of Mick and I, Melinda, Stevo's sister Joy and her young daughter Rebecca. Stevo's sister Mandy and Joy's husband Frank couldn't make it.

Branding itself the world's greatest city of the arts and outdoors, Eugene's 100,000 or so residents live near the Canadian border, south of Washington State on the western side of the continent. Their June summer meant maxes of 22 degrees Celsius (72 degrees Fahrenheit), only just bearable for the cold-hating Sunshine Coasters, so we combined sightseeing with wedding rehearsals, meals with the Raines' clan and the big ceremony at their First United Methodist church.

Groomsman Mick became the instant celebrity in town. It seemed like wherever we went, he would be surrounded by flirting women.

One morning we walked the length of a shopping mall, window browsing and saying g'days, and by the time we came back up the other side all these female assistants and customers were staring from the shopfronts yelling, 'Oooh Mick! Mick from Australia!'

'I remember coming out of a dressing room and here's Mick and Tony with all these girls hovering around them,' Melinda remembers, 'I called out, "Oi! C'mon Tony, he's single but you're not!" The girls must have thought I was a rough Aussie broad.'

'Mick's a good-looking guy, but this reaction was unbelievable. Until it clicked: Mick Dundee. Eugene didn't see many tourists from Down Under, but they all knew Hoge's character from the '80s movie. So sorry ladies, you missed the real Crocodile Hunter!'

In the local bars it didn't take us boys long to discover that American beer was like cordial. Used to drinking XXXX and VB heavies, we threw down Yank brews like Budweiser and demanded, 'What's going on? We need something stronger.'

The barflies were astounded. 'You Aussie boys sure can drink, can't you? You'll have to go to a hard liquor bar.'

A what? We found one of these 'special' pubs and next minute we're drinking bourbon and rum at lunchtime. Once again a group of female admirers gathered to hear Australian Mick's sexy accent.

Each morning we walked across the road from our motel to have brekky at a pancake place that served steaks 24 hours a day. I'm afraid our lack of big-city experience showed.

'How would you like your coffee, sir?' The waitress described 30 flavours.

'Uh, just normal coffee, thanks. Can I have bacon and eggs?'

'How do want your eggs?' She rattled off 20 methods of cooking a goog.

It was all a bewildering joke to us. They certainly take their tucker seriously.

*

Melinda and I really enjoyed the pre-wedding dinner with Terri's extended family at a Mexican restaurant owned by one of her two older sisters. Terri's parents Julia and Clarence couldn't have been nicer or more hospitable. Clarence, a Navy veteran, former policeman and trucking company owner, was both dignified and down-to-earth. (He died aged 86 in June 2008.)

There was a surprising lack of pre-wedding jitters, considering the magnitude of this coming union. Bob, Lyn, Julia and Clarence seemed to get on famously. In fact, I reckon Stevo ended up the only one panicking on the day as he sweated it out in his penguin suit.

It was pretty lucky the bucks' and hens' night was not immediately before the ceremony. We were definitely worse for wear after enjoying colourful bars and strip joints. The funniest part was when the glammed-up girls turned up at the same joint as the boys. We all had an absolute ball—and the boys hitched a ride home in the girls' stretch limo. I'm just glad Stevo didn't give me the ring for safe-keeping until the day of the wedding.

The evening wedding was traditional and meaningful and I was glad to deliver the ring into Stevo's hands without a problem. Melinda was beaming as she helped Terri with her flowing white dress. The knockabout gang from the Sunshine Coast shared a great reception with these two very happy families.

But for the core bunch of bow-tied blokes and frilly chicks, there was an even wilder highlight to come. As you could imagine, the wildlife-obsessive clan couldn't wait to get their hands dirty inspecting the local flora and fauna. Just as soon as my hangover eased...

*

Terri had already given us a tantalising glimpse into American animal rehabilitation methods. Before the wedding she'd shown us through rehab places run by friends such as Cougar Country, a centre she established in her early 20s to save everything from raccoons to horned owls to bobcats. We met her beloved rescued pet cougar Malina at a centre called Wildlife Images and were spellbound by the skills of a grizzly bear handler who had worked for Walt Disney. Stevo and I were wide-eyed as the handler played with this deadly predator like a puppy. Melinda laughed at the irony. To each his own deadly predator, I guess!

After the wedding Bob and Lyn, Stevo and Terri, Clarence and Julia, Mick, Melinda and I visited Crater Lake National Park, about three hours south-east of Eugene. On the way we saw beautiful waterfalls just off the road. Pulling over, Stevo and I couldn't wait to have a drink from them.

But our American hosts shot down that idea, explaining the extent of pollution in some rivers, poisoned by industry. It was one of those moments that made us appreciate Queensland all the more, and vow to protect it.

The national park, however, was serene and pristine. Its dark, lush, volcanic landscape and old-growth plants were very different to Australian flora, although the deep blue lake reminded me of a giant version of Fraser Island's Lake McKenzie.

Then we continued in Clarence's Tarago van to the High Desert Museum, which had sensational animals. Wild cats, otters, raptors, reptiles. Like our park, this zoo started in the '70s with a commitment to environmental education. It was founded by a bloke called Donald who was inspired after he raised a wolf cub.

Terri was in her element on these tours, enjoying our reactions—including our simple delight at feeding squirrels. Of course Stevo made us stop off in the hills behind the museum to search for wild rattlesnakes. A zoo full of them just wasn't enough.

The Irwins were bowled over by the museum's technology, such as push-button units allowing visitors to call up information and pictures for any animal. It had the wow factor and was the stuff of dreams for us.

Another highlight was San Diego Zoo, one of the world's biggest and best, where Bob and Stevo picked up more tips for back home. Walking in, we were blown away to see a herd of giant Galapagos tortoises interacting, even mating.

Stevo couldn't believe the number and size of these ancient creatures, which grow up to 1.8 metres (6 feet) from head to tail. He held out his backpack to indicate scale for this photo (see opposite). He marvelled at the zoo's success in breeding the endangered creatures, something our Harriet never did.

He and Bob gathered as much information as they could for a friend in Queensland, herpetologist Scott Thomson, who was researching Harriet's history and analysing her DNA as a subspecies. Scott, Steve and Terri published the article on Harriet in a US scientific journal in the late '90s.

Land of the giants: Tony with Stevo holding up a backpack to show the enormity of these Galapagos tortoises at San Diego Zoo.

San Diego Zoo also had two beautiful albino Burmese pythons and Caribbean rhinoceros iguanas which have horns on their snouts. We later imported one of those iguanas for our park. Bob didn't exactly show his excitement like Stevo and I did, but we knew he was rapt by the whole experience. I don't think he'd ever been out of Australia.

We were chuffed to note that our standards of animal care were as high, if not higher. In an enclosure where they were breeding mostly Australian reptiles, for example, we noticed mites running all over some Fijian crested iguanas. I could see the endangered lizards scratching at their faces.

'That's bull!' Stevo said. 'How are they breeding them if they're covered in mites? That's risking the rest of their collection too.'

None of us being shy or retiring types, we talked to the workers about their animal husbandry and management. I felt it was a strangely laidback response, 'Oh yeah, they'll be fine.' I knew if mites had got into

Beerwah, especially on rare reptiles, Stevo would have been in there day and night, picking them off one at a time.

The value of sharing conservation knowledge between the countries became obvious to me as we realised the different success rates in breeding programs. Green pythons were responding well to American methods whereas Sulphur-crested cockatoos responded better in Australian zoos. Why? It was that sort of question that young Wes sought answers to when he worked and did research overseas, eventually introducing his new skills back to Australia Zoo after I had left.

The overall experience of interacting so closely with American wildlife had quite an impact on us. We admired the efforts of Oregon carers who formed backyard networks to organise rehabilitation and housing for orphaned or injured species, even the big predators like cougars. I particularly liked the inclusion of raccoons despite their bad rap for ferreting in rubbish bins and attacking house pets.

These volunteer communication networks were more advanced than what Australia was doing at the time, but we also saw holes in their techniques which wouldn't work on our native animals. Aussie species usually suffered worse from stress than exotics.

Many strategies were universal, though. Someone would find a motherless young cub, organise someone to raise it, research its original location including family structures and threats, then organise a suitable release location. Just like any Aussie wildlife carer group.

If you become close to this type of scenario, and feel that sheer joy at helping Mother Nature get back on her feet, it gets into your pores. You want to influence people around you to feel the same.

My kids now harass me all the time about saving animals. We'll be driving on a highway in pitch black and one of them will suddenly say, 'Dad! There's a roo lying by the road!' The other will pipe up, 'Looked like a doe, Dad.' Just to make sure I get the message. So I'll turn the car around, drive back the few kilometres and check on her. Usually she's dead, but sometimes the joey is either still alive in the pouch or struggling to survive after being turfed out by the impact of a bumper bar. The Frisby road trip is postponed until we've rescued the tiny thing and found someone to care for it.

*

Our series of flights en route to Australia proved to be a comedy of errors. First, on the plane to San Diego, we discovered the hazards of not having seat allocations.

At the airport I'd noticed a passerby's enormous build and whispered, 'Have a look at the size of that fella.' The man was very tall and bulging with muscle and fat. I guessed 150 kilograms (330 pounds).

Our group was seated together on the plane, bound for the zoo, when the same man appeared in the cabin. 'This plane's never gonna take off,' I whispered again.

He walked straight to me and said in a broad African American accent, 'You're sitting in my seat.'

I shrugged. There were no numbered tickets and we got there first.

'You're in my and my mother's seats,' he boomed.

I thought, this guy's gonna rip the wing off the plane and belt me with it for sure.

Aloud I said, 'Oh all right then.'

Before I could move, the flight attendant came over and addressed Momma's Boy. 'Something wrong, sir?'

'This man's in my seat,' he said.

'Sir, there are no seat allocations. You'll have to find another seat,' she said.

'There ARE no other seats.' He death-stared me.

We're in trouble here, I thought. Stevo and Mick stared at me. Were we in for a rumble?

Melinda, sitting on the other side of our row, didn't appear too concerned for my welfare.

I looked back at my friends. Now I could see the cracks in their façades. They were trying to control giggles!

Gee, thanks guys.

The hostie at least understood the gravity of the matter, mincing off to the cockpit.

Then the pilot's voice crackled across the intercom. 'We have overbooked. If anyone gets off the plane, we'll give you a free ticket.'

No one moved. The pilot offered the free ticket plus accommodation. Finally someone got off and my acquaintance was able to get a seat. Holy hell, I tell you, it was a worry.

Then, after making it to LA Airport, we lost Stevo. He just goes and goes, until he's exhausted. We'd been up all night because the flights had been messed about. There were more delays.

Suddenly Stevo said, 'I've had enough of this, I'm gonna find somewhere to go to sleep.' He disappeared. Eventually the plane boarded and we waited. They called for him. Again. And again.

We didn't know where he was so the staff had to go find him. He got dirty looks from the other passengers as he ambled on some time later.

Chapter 15

Power shift at work. 'You're not hunting crocs!' Stevo and my friendship in peril. I quit, twice. The sad ritual of Bogie's skull.

Not even a year after they first met, the Irwin newlyweds got back to the park after their honeymoon in north Queensland. So much was changing so quickly.

John Stainton joined Stevo, Terri and Sui on their croc-trapping honeymoon up the Burdekin River. John's footage became *The Crocodile Hunter* series, which was destined to make them international stars when it was picked up by cable TV channel Animal Planet in 1996. It was showing across more than 100 countries in the year Stevo died, 2006.

After Bob and Lyn moved into their rebuilt home at Rosedale, my mate and his new missus started putting their unified stamp on running the show. In 1993 we would all witness the glittering dawn of the re-christened Australia Zoo.

And, slowly but surely, I freaked out.

Initially we all worked well together. Terri and Stevo introduced understandable operational changes as the zoo's popularity surged.

Each day was more thrilling and I revelled in the *oohs* and *ahhs* of the crowds at my croc-feeding demos.

We were so busy keeping up with demand that I had to give up long trips away with Stevo. I just did shorties—collecting or dropping off animals such as Alligator snapping tortoises, cassowaries and Dwarf freshies.

Stevo and I knew something had to be done about the increasing crowd squabbles in the Crocodile Environmental Park as people vied for pole position.

We had tried holding two tours a day in there to spread out the numbers. It stopped working when the crocs got fed up with being fed up.

Staggering the crocs' food intake by ripping off chicken legs instead of using whole carcasses also failed to keep 'em keen. Plus in cooler weather we couldn't feed them much, if at all. Crocs rely on the sun to heat their bodies to aid digestion. If they're not warm enough, the meat rots in their stomachs, poisoning them.

Our next choice was to limit the number of people in that section. But, mate, you should have heard the complaints if a group missed out!

Finally, when we were getting 500 people on weekends, we had to reopen the special croc zone as part of the park. Safety was an issue because the general grounds were only single fenced. If a kid stuck his hand through, it might get bitten off. So we did the hard yakka in double-time to double-fence the whole place.

On the management and administration side, Terri appointed Steve G curator of snakes and me curator of crocodiles. I was pleased with my change of title because that put me on the front line for all the day-to-day stuff to do with crocs. Plus, as you'll recall from my outback adventures, I had no desire to spend extra time with the creepy-crawlies.

Within months, however, I'd had my first blue with Terri in our new roles. I remember it distinctly because it was such a minor start to a major blowout.

When Bob ruled the park, he would walk over to his employees every Friday and hand us our pay packets with a nod and a quiet 'here you go'. That was back in the days when cash-in-hand meant exactly that.

Terri stopped the practice and decided our wages would be paid directly into our bank accounts. Of course that's now the norm, but 16 or so years ago it was unusual and I didn't like it. I wanted my cash. I kicked up a stink and was overruled.

A combination of run-ins followed, mostly over administrative or financial issues—such as Terri wanting to stop bonus payments to staff for getting quotas of people into the Crocodile Environmental Park—but also about animal procedures.

An earlier incident had left me with a sour taste. We'd all argued about how to treat a mature red kangaroo that had gone nuts after a car drove past and broke its foreleg. Terri wanted to fix him. Lyn thought he should be put down.

I understood that Terri probably felt just like Melinda and me in the early days, trying to save every hurt animal. Maybe she also thought the roo would be easier to treat because he lived in the house section of the park. We never put big males near tourists because of their potential aggression. But because I had since learnt the Irwin ways, I agreed with Lyn. I figured Lyn had handraised just about every orphaned roo in the park and it was her call.

Stevo convinced his parents to let Terri have a go. I considered eating my words when Terri's vet wrap bandage appeared to be working. But within weeks the wound was weeping and when the bandage was removed, septicaemia had set in. Stevo went off the Richter scale because we knew the animal had suffered. It was a valuable lesson to us all, really, because we all shared the same soft heart for animals.

Commonsense told me that Terri faced a learning curve while applying her extensive wildlife rehab knowledge to a new situation in a new country, just like she had to put in new business systems to deal with the speed of the park's growth. But my pride was taking a battering.

In hindsight, I started overreacting because I sensed the power shift. I'm not exactly a guy who likes relinquishing power. Things were different and I couldn't accept it. Pigheadedness, ignorance, the curator's curse, call it what you want.

*

It was a nightmare for both the personal and professional sides of my relationship with Stevo. We had done everything together for so long, as friends and workmates, but suddenly someone else was on the scene and I didn't adjust. Sometimes I challenged Stevo to support my opinion even if it conflicted with Terri's. Dumb move, Fris, although he would usually try to find a compromise. On a basic level, I guess I felt like Terri was taking my friend away from me.

I wondered why Stevo let Terri make certain decisions which opposed his previous stances. I questioned his backflips. He became a different beast at work, one that I could no longer predict. My regret is that I couldn't, or wouldn't, see things through Stevo's eyes. He was married to a woman he loved who obviously was going to be central to his life. And his life was his work. I was too self-absorbed to recognise that not only were our trivial arguments just as upsetting for him, he had a hell of a lot more on his plate.

He was also dealing with the normal ups and downs of married life and, having done the same myself, I made sure I was there for him when he needed to talk it out. No one's relationship is without conflict, but at least mates understand.

Stevo and Terri were juggling two career passions: filming their TV series while making grand plans for the zoo. They were extremely busy and an almost volcanic atmosphere pervaded, a sense that the Irwins' popularity was about to explode on to a much wider stage. Stevo realised he had to delegate the smaller croc feeding shows to other staff. He had to focus on growing the business, on dealing with the things most likely to bring in the big money for conservation.

My time was consumed as curator, but sometimes I joined the practicalities of their planning. I helped set up special areas in the park for filming and scouted out appropriate locations on the Coast for documentary scenes.

But I was out of my depth—and not very impressed—with the way some of the publicity stuff was going. Right from the start, actually. I remember standing around the smoko table with Stevo, Lyn, Mandy and Melinda discussing names for the new Steve Irwin public persona. We were resting under a huge Canary Island date palm we called the Tree of Knowledge, watching a little water dragon bobbing his head up and down, and having a laugh at terms like Crocodile Man and Reptile Man (dismissed as too comic strippy). Then 'The Crocodile Hunter' was mentioned.

I burst out, 'No. You're not hunting crocodiles, mate!'

That branding didn't reflect the Stevo I knew—the dedicated leader of our 'bring 'em back alive team' who spent his life preventing people from shooting crocs, even the bad-arse ones, and getting animals to safety in A1 condition. The others tried to persuade me that the name would hook the Americans. As the world now knows, it did. Wrong again, Fris!

*

In more than a brand sense, the Crocodile Hunter phenomenon was the hardest thing that I had to come to grips with. As Stevo became more well-known in the media, money—big money—started to roll in. It was good but…well, there were a few 'buts' in 1993.

What-you-see-is-what-you-get Stevo had never coveted fame or the trappings of success. He was a member of the most genuine, down-to-earth family I knew. Yet there he was, performing and honing his animated technique in front of TV cameras.

It was only exaggerating his natural enthusiasm, but the premeditation and associated publicity seemed so foreign—and funny—to both of us. I rarely missed an opportunity to raise an eyebrow and utter, 'Geez Stevo!' when watching his exuberant practising.

'I'm no actor, Fris!' he'd laugh.

We were all over the moon about the likelihood of his success seriously boosting the coffers of the Irwins' wildlife conservation projects. But Stevo often seemed torn, trying to reconcile with himself the amount of time and effort he spent on the circus side of it.

He told me many times that he considered it a means to an end.

'The Crocodile Hunter and the park are two different entities,' he said. 'I just pour all the money into the park and conservation.' That was the sole reason he accepted such an alien lifestyle.

I don't know if he ever got over this uneasy attitude towards making money. It was just so different to his past. When we were knocking about as teenagers we couldn't have cared less. On those 1980s trips to north and western Queensland we had no budget. Bob paid for our fuel and we paid for our food. That was the scale of it and the beauty of it. The only pressure was whatever we put on ourselves.

Stevo only ever had one dream and that was for people to recognise and respect wildlife. That's it. Even when he was turning over millions, he didn't buy all the best stuff. If you looked in his wardrobe I'd guarantee there weren't many 'good clothes' in it. And he certainly didn't do it for a flash house for himself or Terri. They continued living in Bob and Lyn's old place on the zoo grounds. It wasn't until much later they also bought a canalfront home in the ritzy suburb of Minyama.

Stevo could have owned a Ferrari, but he hated cars. On that wedding trip to Oregon, I'd certainly enjoyed a drive in Terri's cool Corvette. But would Stevo buy one? Not a chance. Why? He couldn't have Sui in a Corvette. And where could he throw his rifle?

He didn't even drive the top class Land Cruisers when he went bush.

It was HiLux every time. When he told me he sank every skerrick of cash into conservation I believed every word. And that's what he did.

*

As Stevo and Terri introduced more rules at the zoo, the demands on staff came thicker and faster. No doubt it was necessary, considering we'd lost three full-time workers—Stevo, Bob and Lyn—as the workload and expectations increased. But the less I understood, the greater my frustration.

Finally I resolved to quit. Well, I think my exact words to Stevo were, 'Well, you can stick your job 'cause I'm not working here anymore.'

I stalked home to the Glass House Mountains. Bob turned up hours later.

'Youse are both pig-headed.' Ra ra ra. 'Turn up to work tomorrow Tony.'

Sure enough, I went back. I respected He Who Must Be Obeyed. Stevo and I were around the 30-mark, but could still act like kids. We flew off the handle at each other then wished it never happened.

For years I suffered migraines. I assumed they stemmed from boxing, but the doctors ended up diagnosing a food allergy, so I stopped eating tomatoes. I'd be working away, raking grass, and all of a sudden I'd break into a hot sweat. Within hours I'd be vomiting and would have to go home, lie down and take tablets to put me to sleep. Sometimes I had to get a needle from the doctor.

If I could get to sleep before I vomited I'd be okay, but once I started, the migraine would get worse because of the heaving. The weirdest part was when I woke up, I felt fine. If it wasn't too late I'd even make it to footy training.

One day I didn't go to work in the morning because of a migraine. The next day I turned up at work with a black eye.

'How'd you get that?' Stevo asked.

'Footy.'

'Oh, so you couldn't come to work but you played footy.'

The blue was on. I think he understood on one level, but I knew it would have sucked for him because there were no staff to cover my chores.

*

In June 1993, a year after we went to the Oregon wedding, Melinda and I quit the zoo and headed north. A few months later I started working for Queensland Parks and Wildlife in Cape York.

I knew I had put Stevo in a really bad spot. Make a decision: support your wife or your mate. You shouldn't do that to people you love.

My last day was pretty gut-wrenching because neither Stevo nor I wanted to sever the tie, but I felt my place was no longer there. We both had to look to the future, not the past.

It happened while we were doing the daily clean. Plain and simple, Stevo and I had words and I walked out. A little while later Melinda went to talk to him.

Melinda remembers: 'Steve said, "Do what you have to do," and of course that was to support my husband for whatever reason. Back home, Tony and I started packing.'

A week or so later Stevo turned up at our shed at Glass House with a surprising request. 'Can I have Bogie's head back?'

I agreed and handed it over.

But that ol' croc skull meant a lot to me. Bogie was the 13-footer (4 metres) we'd brought back from Bowen River.

When the croc died Stevo had said, 'Would you like the head?'

'You bet I would.' Bogie was one of the biggest animals that I'd ever caught.

'Well, you'll have to get it, I can't.'

'All right, no worries.'

I'd been flat out just picking up the head, which probably weighed

40 kilograms (more than 80 pounds). But it was something I could keep to symbolise our experiences. I'd taken it home, built a fire, put it in a drum and boiled off all the flesh to leave a clean skull.

Its return was the saddest ritual. So much was unspoken between Stevo and me. In fact we didn't discuss it until years later. He then revealed, 'I cried for a couple of days, Fris. I couldn't believe we weren't doing what we did any more.'

Not long after my departure, Steve G left, Wes returned and over the next decade Australia Zoo's fame skyrocketed as TV celebrity Steve Irwin became a household name from the Sunshine Coast in Queensland to the Sunshine Coast in Canada.

Chapter 16

A new conservation niche. We're baa-aack. Pot-stirring at the zoo. Mates miss the Caloundra boy made good. Influence lingers.

Stevo and I didn't have a proper conversation for up to 12 months. I was 29 and immature. He was disappointed and busy. It was my first extended period without crazy Stevo slamming through my life since I was a youngster. I felt guilty for leaving and for failing to understand the full picture of what was happening in his life. We had separate jobs, separate families and lived 1900 kilometres (1200 miles) apart. It hurt.

People always ask me if I regret leaving the park. My answer remains: in those circumstances, no. I admitted that to Stevo too, many years later, after people we knew had suffered marriage breakups and personal crises.

Put simply, working at the park meant an extraordinary commitment, regardless of your skill level, family situation or pay packet. It was not a nine to five, five day a week job. Stevo did not hide the fact he expected his colleagues to share his obsession. Forget external sports or hobbies, if Stevo was eating, living and sleeping the zoo, you should be too.

Having already suffered under the stresses of change, I'd decided to make a more stable, balanced life for my wife and the two wonderful children we had. Hypothetically, if I had stuck around I might have remained Stevo's right-hand-man and travelled the world on more Irwin adventures. But would the continuous upheaval have been worth risking my marriage and children? I don't think so.

I make no bones about the fact that some of my behaviour was stupid. I wish it had not caused such a separation in our friendship.

If I look objectively at the progress of the zoo since then, it's obvious that I had taken things as far as I could, passing on the skills I had learnt at Hartley's Creek. When Stevo found Terri she took it to an all-new level. Now that Stevo is gone, the zoo is aiming for new heights.

*

By late 1994 Stevo and I were in contact. Our shared passion for wildlife of course had not dimmed and neither had our camaraderie, albeit from a distance. I guess to a degree, time heals.

I was a ranger in Cooktown and a member of the Cape York Crocodile Advisory Group when it was decided that we would hold a croc awareness week for the local kids. So it seemed natural for me to ring Stevo, who was idolised by the kids. It proved our ice-breaker. He donated more than 300 awareness kits when he realised he wouldn't be able to change his commitments to attend the function.

I loved working full-time in that incredible environment. We surveyed croc numbers and relocated those that threatened built-up areas. We helped raise awareness among Aboriginal communities about their traditional use of turtles, crocs and dugong and liaised with Indigenous rangers in park management.

I was also involved in the protection of Foxtail palms, a vulnerable species. These palms, which grow only in the Melville Range on Cape York, are up to 15 metres (50 feet) tall with plume-like leaves, greeny flowers and red fruit. Keen gardeners love them. They're highly prized by nurseries and plant collectors and we had a real problem with illegal seed collection threatening the existing stocks.

Over the next decade my friendship with Stevo remained, but it mostly operated on the backburner. You know, those friends you have who live far away, but whenever you finally speak all the memories and closeness come flooding back?

Stevo was the same person and did the same things but all of a sudden he was a megastar—and mega-busy. He was in Africa, Antarctica, the Himalayas. He was upgrading the zoo's exhibits, away catching crocs, launching the Wildlife Warriors Worldwide conservation foundation, starring in his TV series and filming in his 2002 feature movie. His daughter Bindi Sue was born in July 1998 and his son Robert Clarence in December 2003.

I loved the given names for his daughter. Stevo always enjoyed naming the crocodiles in the park and Bindi was a female saltie, just over 2-metres (6.5-feet) long, that we'd brought back from a crocodile farm at Babinda about 1990. Sue was presumably close to Sui, his canine companion.

Magical moments came during our infrequent face-to-face visits. I practically gave up on phone calls. It was a bitter pill to make appointments with my old mate through personal assistants. I didn't like leaving messages with someone I'd never met.

Sometimes on these visits the emotion was overwhelming. Stevo and I shed a fair few nostalgic tears. We wished we hadn't let external stuff get the better of us. Then he'd spark up, excitedly taking my family through his house, showing us his latest zoo animals.

At one enclosure he said in delight, 'Jump in here with the alligators, have a look at that big male.'

So Melinda, Sheyanne, Nathan and I jumped in and chatted to Stevo in the enclosure. I turned around. 'Holy hell.'

A huge crowd of people was watching us. Stevo talked into a radio set as staff swarmed around our enclosure.

'What is going on, Steve?'

He explained that he had to wear disguises if he wanted to walk undetected around the zoo.

'What a load of bull Steve, what are you doing?' I said.

'Listen mate, this is the way it is now,' he said.

He organised some employees to look after my family all day while he came and went according to duties. At the croc-feeding show he always referred to us.

'See the Frisbys up there in the stand? They helped build this park. Tony helped catch most of the crocodiles in here.'

Yep, it made me feel good.

*

I couldn't go a whole visit without making mischief though. Melinda berated me if I tried to gee up the staff, but what the hell. I dodged our escort and walked past a pond calling, 'Acco, c'mon Acco,' to see if the saltie remembered my voice. He came right over.

An angry keeper appeared. 'Don't harass that crocodile, mate.' Then I'd do the same with Mary.

Probably my favourite was seeing a poor guy mowing the enclosures. That old chestnut. 'Get down closer to it, mate, what's wrong with you?', I called out.

'How would you like to do this?'

'Sure, no worries.' I put my hands on the fence to jump over.

'Don't come in here!' he yelled at me…and don't be such a stirrer, Melinda added.

Then Stevo would rock up. 'Fris, you stirring up my staff again?'

After a while, the keepers all got to know when the Frisbys were coming so they could prepare. I told Stevo I was just being a smart arse because I could see the crew of young guys were doing a decent job.

However I was surprised by the new methods and rules.

'Workplace health and safety these days, Fris,' he said. 'None of my staff are allowed to touch the water or the animals or get within a certain distance of the crocs.'

'Gee, that would make it a bit boring,' I said.

'Well, that's why people like it when I do the shows. I don't abide by the rules!' Good ol' Stevo.

Occasionally his natural optimism slipped and he confided in me about the underbelly of fame. He hated false people and I watched him make excuses not to be somewhere or not to do something. But his greatest fear was for the safety of his children.

On a visit about 2000, I remember walking through the gate into a new breeding snake shed near the house so Stevo could show me his new baby brood, rare green pythons.

'Fris, I'd give anything to have your life,' he said. 'Everyone wants a piece of me and everyone wants me for something other than me. I'm worried about the kids. We're getting threats that the kids are going to get abducted. I meet with the chief of police and security and all this stuff.'

'Are you kidding or what?' I was shocked.

'No, that's what it's like.'

Stevo's unyielding love for his kids is the reason why he was so shattered in January 2004 when he was publicly condemned for holding baby Bob while feeding a croc at the zoo. He was horrified that critics put him in the same league as pop star Michael Jackson, who had held his child over a balcony. Only days before, my family and my sister Mandy's family had enjoyed a wonderful visit to the zoo. We'd watched Stevo dote on his newborn son and shared his joy. My mate was a proud, caring father.

*

Many of Stevo's mates missed his company enormously when he hit the big-time. The few that I could fit in this book are the tip of a friendship iceberg. As Di Schwenke says, none of us begrudged his extraordinary success and we realised Steve was focusing on raising a young family, just as we all did. 'We were proud of the Caloundra boy made good,' Di says. 'It was just a bit sad because we felt neglected, like we'd lost him to celebrity status.'

The Schwenkes hadn't seen Steve for five years when they wandered through Australia Zoo in April 2004. 'We wanted to have a gander at what he'd done,' said Rob. 'Suddenly Di yelled, "Here he comes."

'I stuck my finger out as he rode past on this bike, security guards front and back telling us to back off. When he recognised us I teased, "Have a go at you, the Crocodile Hunter's blushing."

'Steve asked, "Have youse got time to come and see my world?" We spent the rest of the afternoon and evening with him, from the tiger cubs and the grandstand to meeting Terri, Bindi and baby Robert at their place. Steve talked and talked, about Caloundra, who he was. He was never a bragger, he just described what it was like being friends with actors like Will Smith and Cameron Diaz, scientists and heads of state.

'I said, "So what's the Croc Hunter drinking on a Friday night?" He opened the fridge and we laughed at the chocolate milk and Coca-Cola. Not one beer to be seen. I guessed that a countery at the local pub was out of the question.'

'It made us feel good,' says Di, 'because you could see part of Steve would still love to shed the *famous* jacket and revisit the old days, his old network. He knew what he'd achieved was amazing and he seemed pretty content. He and Bindi had such a close affinity. She had impeccable manners and you could see her intelligence.'

Today, Rob says he's glad he got the chance that night to tell Steve how much he was missed and how the wild times of Caloundra had shaped him. 'His time was precious but I know he occasionally caught up with Micky and Rod. I think we all figured that when he turned 50 and slipped out of the limelight we'd see more of him. We always knew Steve was an amazing character, but he was just one of the boys. It's so weird to drive down the Bruce Highway in 2009 and see him sitting up there on that billboard (advertising the zoo).

'Steve was bigger than life and we thought he would be here forever. That day he died made me question life in general. I thought, "Hey this mortality thing is real."'

*

Jibba points to Steve's influence on many of us, whether it was his grab-life-by-the-balls personality or his passion for conservation. Jibba says, 'I knew Steve well from when he was doing his diesel mechanic apprenticeship at Maroochy Council, then when he left the council and got the park going while doing the contract work up north. The environmental stuff brushed off on to Tony and Mick, who both ended up working for the Parks and Wildlife Service. I saw how close Steve and Tony got, especially when Tony started getting into the wildlife projects. Tony only left the park because of that personality or power clash.

'Most of us hardly saw Steve after he got married and started doing his documentary series while turning the park into Australia Zoo. He was always invited to everyone's birthdays and weddings but rarely made one. He came to my 30th but not my 40th, for example. I would call his parents' house, which became the zoo's number, but I never knew if the messages got through. When I did run into him he'd always ask about the other guys because he knew how impossible his schedule was. I don't reckon he changed much—except for the security guards.'

Chris White continues. 'After he got married I only really saw Steve when I took the family to the zoo and we'd all have lunch, or at functions after I was elected to Caloundra Council in the early 2000s. I remember when Steve and Terri opened the enormous Crocoseum. Steve would ask, "How you going Whitey?" but he didn't have time to listen. His fame didn't let him be who he used to be. How he grew up is what made Steve, but in the end he just had too much on his plate. It was a shame because our families had been so close and my parents had thought the world of him. I just wished Steve could go and say g'day to them.

'It wasn't until I was sitting with my daughters in the VIP section at the public memorial after his death that our family truly realised how many people Steve had touched, other than his Caloundra mates.'

*

I reckon Stevo knew that, to some extent, the hassles of his fame were a necessary evil. He had more insight and foresight than me: he knew the celebrity mantle was a means of reaching millions of people with the conservation message. It wasn't just entertainment, it spread his passion and love for the environment and wildlife. On TV screens, his message would live forever. So would he.

Chapter 17

Shock news from the Coastguard. Why Stevo inspires. If we can convince one person...

In 2002, I had to smile at the irony of Stevo starring in a hit movie. *The Crocodile Hunter: Collision Course* co-starred Terri and was directed by John Stainton.

I'd never known Stevo to sit still long enough to watch a movie, let alone act in one. He couldn't and wouldn't. I think as a teenager he took girlfriends to the pictures a couple of times, but undoubtedly had an ulterior motive.

And while I don't think we ever saw *Crocodile Dundee* when it came out in the '80s, Stevo loved to milk the line, 'That's not a knife, this is a knife.' He carried a massive razor-sharp knife to use in the mangroves. It was his tool for slashing branches and roots to build barriers around the traps so crocs couldn't sneak bait from the sides.

That October, during what would be one of our last visits with Stevo at the zoo, when my son Natty and I joined Bindi and him in the Komodo dragon enclosure, he compiled a wonderful DVD and gave us a copy.

A now-poignant photo of our families together at the zoo.

In 2005, bitten by nostalgia, I raised the possibility of returning to the zoo's staff. Stevo, who by then delegated all operational matters, suggested I ask Wes about vacancies.

I never pursued it. My own job was filled with wildlife adventures, my family was settled and content, and I realised that going back might fall far short of my expectations.

On 4 September 2006, I was fishing with my dad John in our boat about 30 nautical miles off Yeppoon. The conditions were beautiful, dead flat and the tides were right in the afternoon, so I suggested we stay overnight. I radioed the Coastguard to ask him to ring my mum and tell her that Dad and I were staying out.

Minutes later the Coastguard relayed an odd message from Mum.

'Tony, the person that you were best man for has died and you need to come home.'

I couldn't work it out. I'd been best man for two mates, Clive and Stevo. I'd never lost anyone close.

We were still two hours' run back to the marina. When I eventually learnt she meant Stevo I simply didn't believe it. He was invincible. Mum had talked in code because she'd only been informed via our closeknit group and had no official confirmation.

It didn't sink in until a few days later when I walked into my backyard aviary, where I usually doted on two parrots worth a couple of thousand bucks. I put seed in their containers and walked out. I left the door wide open. I never saw either bird again. They had two babies in the nest. I broke down.

Media reports of Steve Irwin's sudden death at 44 caused shockwaves and an outpouring of grief not just across Queensland, but around Australia and the world. The public could barely fathom that the famous, fearless Crocodile Hunter, larrikin legend and wildlife warrior, had fallen victim to a stingray barb to the chest while swimming in shallow water on the Great Barrier Reef, filming another doco.

His hometown newspaper, the *Sunshine Coast Daily,* reported how the injured 'TV star and naturalist' had been pulled aboard his research vessel, Croc One, for a 30-minute emergency dash to meet a rescue chopper. The article continued: 'The crew of Croc One performed constant CPR during the voyage to Low Isle but medical staff pronounced Irwin dead about noon. His body was flown to a morgue in Cairns, where stunned family and friends were gathering.'

Local and global reactions proved the enormity of Stevo's influence. Tributes ranged from young fans at Beerwah to the Australian Prime Minister's Office and from America to Britain. As a spontaneous remembrance wall of khaki and flowers formed at the zoo's entrance, there were dedicated websites, television specials, celebrity and political speeches. An executive for the Wildlife Warriors organisation, quoted in the *Sunshine Coast Daily*, said the messages of support, flowers and donations had been so overwhelming it resembled 'a Lady Di moment'.

On 20 September, a capacity crowd of 5500 attended a public memorial at the zoo, where little Bindi's words of devotion upstaged even Aussie entertainer John Williamson's performance and messages from Hollywood stars Cameron Diaz and Russell Crowe.

However, all I could think about were the times we laid our lives on the line for each other. Now his was snuffed out. We had dealt with so much physical danger, from risky sports and outback encounters to dumb teen fights. How could this have happened?

I kept hearing him say, 'Isn't she a little beauty?' about his baby girl Bindi.

I could still look at my darling daughter Sheyanne, caring for her pet parrots.

Memories. Joy and sorrow. I reckon Stevo's greatest joys were his kids and animals. His greatest sorrow was the death of his mum Lyn. When her car accident happened in 2000, his life was in overdrive, I was living in Cooktown and my attempt to reach him failed. There was not a lot I could do, I guess, but I knew the emotional impact it had on him. And Bob.

*

What I learnt from the Irwins will never leave me. To this day I'm involved in crocodile activities, surveying their numbers and behaviour in Shoalwater Bay for the Department of Defence. The bay is used by Aussie and American military for training exercises, so the data must be accurate and up-to-date.

I'm pleased that government authorities now realise the Irwins' contribution to conservation, following the Beerwah park's occasionally uneasy relationship with them in the 1980s. Something to do with regulations and original techniques.

I'm stoked that Stevo's contributions to research and science have been recognised, such as his project to install and track satellite transmitters in crocs up north in Lakefield National Park. I love the fact that academics respect his knowledge, considering he didn't do any formal training and made some discoveries by accident.

The proudest scientific moment I shared with Stevo was finding that rare canopy goanna at Iron Range. And I was quietly stoked to have accompanied him on a croc survey trip to the Burdekin River about 1990 when we spotted a new species of turtle near a weir. It was a strange, white-headed, snapping turtle which we caught and released, not realising its significance. When Stevo returned to the area with Bob, they hooked one on fishing line and sent photos back to researchers. It was an unknown species that even got named after them—the *Elseya Irwini*.

I reckon Stevo was born with a scientist's mind. He was always studying animals, noticing differences, comparing behaviour. Remember in the Burdekin, when he was fascinated by crocs that had four scutes on the neck instead of six? He was adamant it was a regional subspecies. The experts didn't subspeciate them, saying it could be an aberration or a matter of environmental adaptation. This may simply be a matter of time.

It just goes to show that anyone with an interest in wildlife should pursue their dreams with all their heart, because you never know what you might discover or where it might lead. That's what I always said to Stevo about talking to crowds at the park.

'If we can convince one person in that crowd, and they develop a dedication to wildlife after it, we've won. Every week let's get one more person.'

For example I became mates with a copper in north Queensland years ago when he lived by the adage: the only good snake is a dead snake. Now he actually pulls snakes off country roads when he's doing night patrol. Even when his team does drug raids on rural properties he calls the Parks department to care for any pet reptiles. Once when I was working for Parks up there he allowed me to wake him at 3am to help load a croc out of a boat into the back of a ute. In darkness, out the back of the police station, he helped wet it down while we waited for transport.

You'd be surprised at the number of people who change their whole outlook on animals after a little interaction or demonstration.

I not only felt privileged to learn about wildlife from the master—and his parents—but I also got to party with him! Have you ever noticed the way 'ir-win' is tucked up in the word 'whirlwind'? I'm so glad to have been sucked into it.

Melinda and I recently took our two children to visit Bob, who has built an amazing new life with his wife Judy on the massive property near Kingaroy. We also attended an emotional surprise birthday party for him, spending a chilly night of nostalgia and bush poetry around the blazing campfire at his new Camp Chilli. It's gratifying and heart-wrenching to see him. The deaths of his wife and son and fallout with his daughter-in-law Terri and two grandchildren have taken their toll. How much can one poor man take?

But the resilience and stubbornness I saw in him years ago has already resurfaced. This man of 70 lived in a tent with no water or electricity on his property in winter 2008 so he could build a high electric fence to protect the kangaroos from dingoes.

My hope for my old stomping ground is that Australia Zoo continues to focus on animal welfare. Surely they don't need to get sidetracked into resort accommodation, celebrity hypnotists or music events. Although, I've been wrong before!

*

After reliving the ups and downs for this book, I still wonder why it took money and fame to make Steve Irwin. It angers me that people think his only impact on crocodile conservation occurred after TV cameras taped it.

He didn't go to acting school to portray an adventurer and wildlife saviour, he'd performed such feats in real life since he was a kid. Why didn't the experts and authorities recognise this earlier? Why didn't they back the Irwins' conservation efforts before dollar signs dangled?

It's a shame to think that millions more Americans than Australians appreciated Stevo and his efforts. It's a greater shame that he became more revered after he died.

If he'd had more local support while he was alive, Stevo could have made a greater impact on controversial Aussie environmental issues, such as banning crocodile farming. Did you know he bought up a heap of land tracts not only on Cape York, but in south-western Queensland and down in Tasmania? The purchases weren't for profit, they were for wildlife reserves. On his land near Blackbutt he planted eucalypt trees for food for koala populations, now under dire threat of extinction due to disease and habitat destruction. On his land near St George he dug dams so wildlife had water in the drought.

When he got involved in all those overseas conservation projects, I'd ask why he didn't do more agitating in Australia. His answer? 'Because they don't want to listen.'

In my eyes, if the Crocodile Hunter had never surfaced Stevo would still be walking on water. He helped save countless reptiles and inspired everyone who knew him, long before he was the Crocodile Hunter. His amazing deeds started as a kid and they should now inspire kids of future generations into feeling just as passionate about protecting native animals.

That's why I wanted this story told.

And that's why my son Natty already has a pet snake.

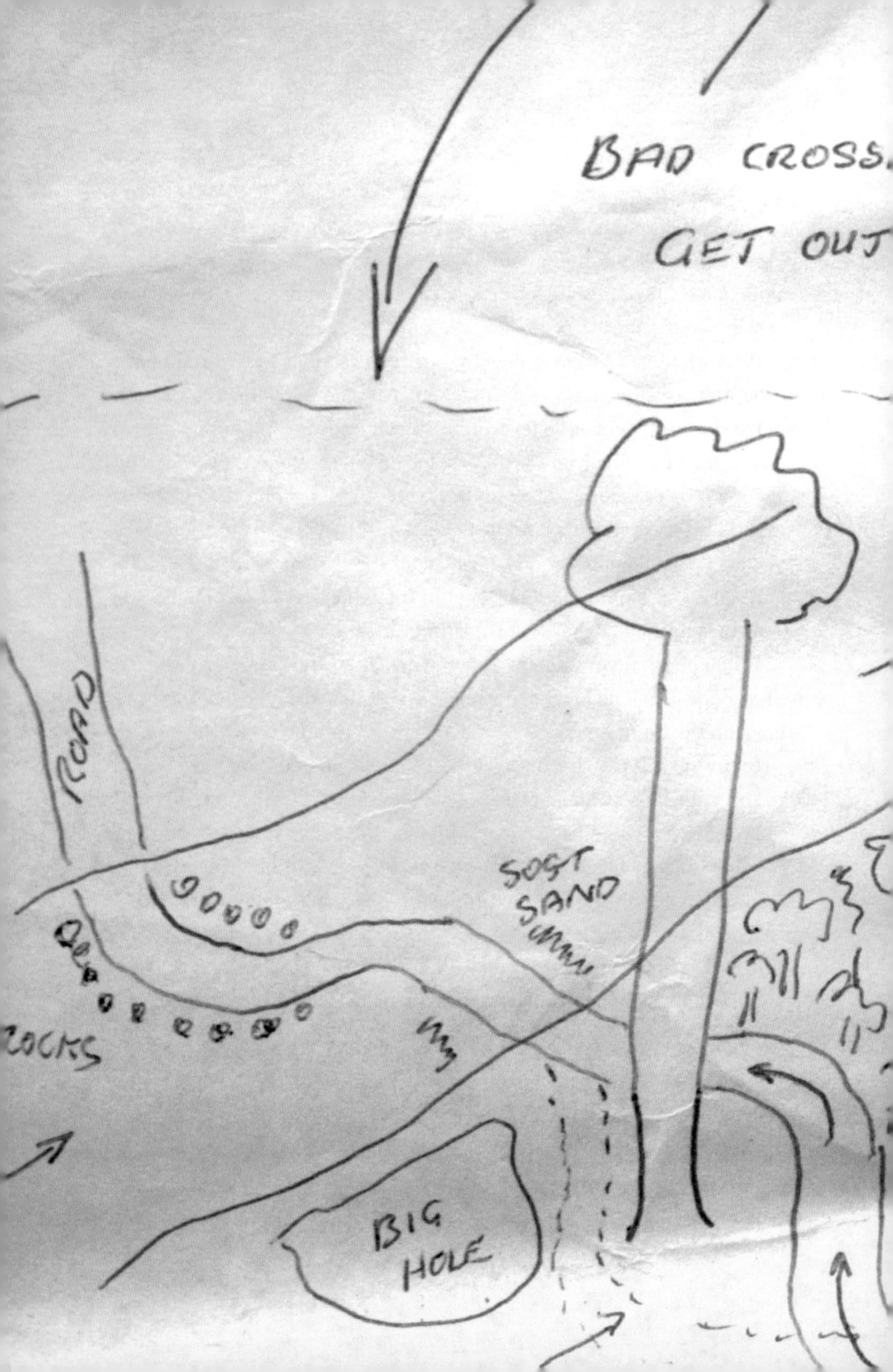
BAD CROSS.
GET OUT
ROAD
SOFT SAND
ROCKS
BIG HOLE

Glossary of our slang

A session—a drinking session
All over the shop—going in all directions
Bag—as a verb, criticise or condemn
Barfly—regular patron at a bar
Beer o'clock—good time for a drink, could be any tick of the clock
Bevvie—beverage, as in beer
Blue—have a fight or make a mistake
Boardie—boardshort, swimsuit for men
Bottl'o—bottle shop selling alcohol
Brekky—breakfast
Bundy Rum—Bundaberg Rum, a famous Aussie spirit made from molasses in Queensland's sugarcane region
Bung—injured, not in good working order
Bushie—local living in the outback, often bearded and dry-humoured
Caned—like 'thrashed', defeated overwhelmingly
Choice joint—nice place
Cop/copped—as a verb it means 'to suffer' some affliction
Copper—policeman
Cost a pretty penny—paid a lot of money
Countery—counter meal at a pub, often steak and chips
Dodgy—dubious, tricky
Esky—portable cold boxe for storing ham sangas and bevvies
Fair sort—attractive woman

Fanged—sank fangs into
Gave us the drum—laid down the house rules
Gee up—tease, provoke
Glammed-up—dressed glamorously
Goog—egg
Grog—beer
Hostie—air hostess, flight attendant
In the black—financially free of debt, opposite of 'in the red'
Legged it—ran fast
Make no bones about it—I'm speaking the truth; don't dispute it
Murri—Indigenous Queenslander
Nutters—silly, crazy people
Ocker—knockabout Aussie
On the seat of our pants—barely staying 'in the black' financially
On the turps—drink alcohol (word play on turpentine)
Pack up its ol' kit bag—move on, from an old wartime marching song
Packing death —extremely frightened
Pulling chicks—attracting the ladies, getting dates
Rapt—stoked, delighted
Rollie—roll your own cigarette, filters optional
Sanga—sandwich
Save my bacon—save my skin, my life
Servo—service station where petrol is sold
Shot the breeze—chatted idly
Silly buggers—mucking around, playing mischievously
Slip slop slap—catchy 1980s advertising campaign by Cancer Council Australia which encouraged us to slip on a shirt, slop on sunscreen and slap on a hat to protect against sun damage to our skin
Spottie—spotlight
Stick that in your pipe and smoke it—a challenge: you may not like what I'm saying but you better believe it. And if you doubt me, you'll eat your words

Stoked—delighted, rapt, ecstatic, used often by Aussie surfers
Stubby—or stubbie, a beer bottle smaller than a longneck or tallie; Stubbies is also the brandname of a clothing company
Tie one on—drink alcohol
Tinnie—small, open, aluminium runabout or boat, popular with fishermen (Brisbane has an annual Tinnie & Tackle Show); tinnie can also mean a can of beer
Tucker—food

KADAMPA BUDHIST TEMPLE
17-19 Apr.

The Bob Irwin Wildlife Fund

The Bob Irwin Wildlife Fund is a not-for-profit conservation organisation affiliated with the Royal Society for the Prevention of Cruelty to Animals (RSPCA) Queensland, which is dedicated to the preservation of all wildlife and its habitat for future generations.

To find out more, or to donate, go to:
www.bobirwinwildlife.com